PILLARS of AWESOME RELATIONSHIPS

HOW TO LOVE YOUR MAN WHEN YOU ARE READY TO KILL HIM

BY

MARCUS AMBRESTER

This book is dedicated to:

Celia and Roy Ambrester for saying "yes" in 1970;

Joe Gentry for showing me how to see with more
than my eyes in 1986;

Leo Droppleman for teaching me to pay attention in 1989;

Steve Citty for saying "no" in 1998;

Cheryl Rose Patterson for giving me flight in 1999;

Jennilea Ambrester for agreeing to an
80-year commitment in 2000;

Duey Freeman for showing me what's possible in 2001; and to

Bug and JoJo,
that you may have a better world in which to live.

CONTENTS

Preface vii

Introduction ix

Part One: *The Four Pillars of Awesome Relationships*

Chapter 1: It's Not About Joy or Pain, but Intensity 3

Chapter 2: Bright Lights Cast Dark Shadows 13

Chapter 3: Hurt Feelings Are Like Rowdy Teenagers........................ 23

Chapter 4: Love Is Not About Your Beloved—Love Is
Feeling the Heart of God................................. 33

Part Two: *The 12 Most Common Pitfalls of Relationships*

Chapter 5: Is the World Okay?................................... 53

Chapter 6: Am I Okay?................................... 65

Chapter 7: Saying "No"................................... 81

Chapter 8: Saying "Yes" 97

Chapter 9: Take a Breath................................... 111

Chapter 10: Responsibility and Blame 119

Chapter 11: Listening 127

Chapter 12: Integrity 135

Chapter 13: Housework 145

Chapter 14: Inspiring Your Man vs. Emasculating Your Man............... 161

Chapter 15: Love Your Sexuality 173

Chapter 16: You Can Be Right or You Can Be Happy 185

About the Author 195

Acknowledgments 197

PREFACE

Experience is the best teacher. I wish I could tell you that I was born a relationship master with a vision of the incredible possibilities that relationships offer us, and that I wrote this book to share that vision with you. The truth is that I was born wounded with a heart imprinted with rejection and abandonment. I was adopted at birth and carried psychic pain from both my birth mother and my birth father, leaving me feeling broken for many years.

When I write in these pages that it is possible to heal, I mean it—I've lived it. I have struggled to heal for myself every hurt described in this book in one way or another, and I've committed every relationship foul I caution you here not to commit. I am a human being, and as good as it feels to offer this great work to you, it doesn't make me any better than you. I just happen to be the guy who got the call to write this one.

I only ever wanted to be three things in my life: a good father, a good husband, and a good coach. I don't know how good I am at any of them, but I can tell you this: I wake up every morning and go to bed every night thankful for my incredible wife, my adorable and funny children, and the dedicated clients and students who trust me to guide them on their journey. I am privileged and thankful to be able to sit with people who are in pain, asking for my help, and to share what I have learned. It is of great comfort to have found my spiritual path, which enables me to meet people in those darkest of places where they feel lost and not lose my bearings and feel lost myself.

If you find any wisdom or truth in these pages, and it helps you to heal and brings you closer to your beloved, I'm honored to have helped. The work isn't always easy, and you should pat yourself on the back for the work you have already done and the continued growth you are doing.

Introduction

Are you longing for emotional intimacy? Would you like the skills to turn conflict into closeness? Did you start off with a great connection with your partner? Do you feel like your connection has been lost and replaced with a mountain of hurt, frustration, anger, and resentment? This book is all about creating intimacy on the emotional, spiritual, and physical levels and learning how to turn disagreements into understanding and acceptance so that your relationship can be a blessing on your sacred journey.

We all make decisions a thousand times a day that enable us to get emotionally closer to, move further away from, or maintain the status quo with others. In this book, you'll learn the emotional and communications skills necessary to create closer, more intimate relationships while maintaining healthy boundaries. You'll also learn why people—and this could mean you—would choose to live and relate in ways that *don't* work. You will learn the tools to getting greater clarity about who you really are and how to share who you truly are in relationships. And finally, you will also learn how to keep from falling into the most common pitfalls of romantic relationships, giving you an even greater chance to make your relationships flourish. If you have no idea what any of this means, then reading this book will *definitely* move you in the right direction!

I am a firm believer that the only way to teach emotional closeness is by meeting a person exactly where that person is emotionally and speaking to his or her heart exactly where it is. I always cracked up when people told me that I should write a book. "Marcus," they'd say, "there are thousands, *millions* of people who need what you teach." I always responded with, "What I teach is coming out specifically tailored to you. When we are talking, the important parts that you need to hear come out because you need to hear them, and they come out *how* you need to hear them. There's no way anyone could get a customized learning experience like this by reading a book." This is so true!

What I *can* do, though, is offer you a book that can lead you to your own customized learning experience. We'll have to do this differently than we would if we were sitting face-to-face, but let's give it a shot.

Since we are not sitting and sharing, I don't have the context of what is going on in your life. I know *what* you need to hear, but I don't know *how* you need to hear it or how you will be able to hear it. This book is not a substitute for making direct heart-to-heart contact with another human being and it is not a substitute for doing one of my workshops. My intention is to help you learn to make heart-to-heart contact—but this book alone cannot do that for you. This book can only point you in the right direction.

So here you are reading a book that is quite possibly the most important book you will ever read, and just by virtue of the fact that you are reading a book instead of relating face-to-face with another human, you're in the paradox of reading "about" other people's experiences—and only thinking about your own experiences. In this book, I will tell you what direction to take your awareness, but this book cannot coach you and guide you the way an experienced relationship coach or therapist can. So you may want to consider attending one of my workshops or working with a coach or therapist to fully integrate what you're learning here.

This book *will* get you excited and motivated to confront the problems you have avoided up until now. This book will also get you excited to heal the hurts that have held you back and give you the tools you need to make your relationships awesome.

It Is Never Too Late

It is never too late to make your relationship awesome. Here is one of my favorite examples of that. An adorable couple, each of them 72 years young, once came into my office because they realized that after 43 years of marriage, they could make their relationship better. They adored each other and each felt that the other's presence in his or her life had been a personal and spiritual blessing.

She was a world-class worrier, and her worry lead to debilitating anxiety on a weekly basis. He was a happy-go-lucky guy, except when confronted with her anxiety.

"When she begins to worry and 'fall into the worry hole,' I get frustrated," he shared. "I shouldn't. I shouldn't get frustrated. But I don't understand *why* she chooses to see things the way she does. I just want to know *why*. I don't understand."

As I began to probe, he added, "This is the most wonderful woman I know—that I have ever known! I just hate it when she falls down into that [worry] hole." When he gets frustrated, he talks to her in a gruff, angry way. He begins to tell her to stop thinking the way she is thinking and then he tells her how she should be thinking about things. When he does this, she starts feeling abandoned, which only adds to her worry.

When the two of them first came into my office, she was in tears because she felt all alone when she began to worry about something. I redirected him to feel his love for her and communicate from that loving place. When he did, he began to feel his love for his wife of 43 years, which was a very sweet, tender love; his frustration began to melt away. His face changed from frustrated to warm. He began to tear up, and I asked him to look her in the eye and repeat what seemed like the powerful part of what he had said: "You are the most wonderful woman I have ever known." As he repeated this, her face changed, too. Her body relaxed and all the stress seemed to drain out of her.

I asked him to imagine that he was a huge, over-stuffed down comforter made of pure love that she could lean back into and be wrapped up in to feel held. When he began to feel *only* his love and stopped trying to "fix" what she was worried about, he began to fix the real issue! The issue that needed to be addressed was not her worry. The *real* issue was feeling connected to each other. When she worries, she doesn't feel her connection to him; she doesn't feel anything but fear. And when he gets frustrated with her worry, he isn't feeling his love for her.

It was easy for them to connect with the love they had for each other. They simply needed the skills to connect with that love in sticky situations. So many couples start off like this couple, with an incredible connection, only to feel as though their connection gets lost from time to time.

How to Get the Most Out of Your Investment

Now that you've invested the money to buy this book and you're about to invest the time to read it, how can you capitalize on your investment to get the most out of it? I have three suggestions. First, accept responsibility for looking inside your own heart and your own experience and make this book your own. Look at the places in your life where the principles apply to you (all of them will, to some degree). Here are some questions for reflection:

- Where in your life do you say "yes" and go deeper into relationship?
- Where do you say "no"?
- When do you feel the presence of God/Spirit/ Higher Power blessing your relationships?
- When do you notice swings from closeness to distance?
- When do you feel frustrated because your partner "doesn't get it"?
- When do you say "no" when you need to say "yes"?
- When do you say "yes" when you need to say "no"?
- When do you keep silent in a conversation and still have something to add?
- When do you listen to your feelings, and when do you shut down?
- When have you ended a relationship and looked back only to see that disturbing indicators existed early on, but you ignored them?
- When problems occur in your relationship, how do you cope with the discomfort?
- How important is it for you to be right?

These are just a few questions that I want you to pay attention to while you're reading this book.

Second, keep a journal of all the questions and the stories that pop into your head. This will help you to be more actively engaged in your process. Pay particular attention to the stories that you would rather forget. I call them "Don't Go There" places. Our "Don't Go There" places hold the deepest pain and often the deepest shame. When those hurts are healed, our heart feels more free than we ever thought possible.

Third, be willing to see your challenges as opportunities. The skills and perspectives you are about to learn are the tools you need to remain feeling truly connected with your partner and to stop dreading the occasions when someone's anger or hurt catches you off guard. You will come to see those times as an incredible opportunity to "step in" closer in your relationship and to bring your full presence to the situation rather than pulling back in hurt or frustration. This mindset matters, and the more you can adopt it the more success you will experience.

Four Words *Not* to Get Hung Up On

Throughout this book, I use four important words that many people always seem get hung up on: *intimacy*, *chemistry*, *skills*, and *God*. I want to discuss them briefly here.

Intimacy: This word is used in our culture mostly as a code word for sexual intercourse. When I use the word "intimacy," I am not talking about sex. When I talk about sex or sexuality, I use the word "sex." What I mean by intimacy is emotional closeness—letting someone get close to you emotionally and letting yourself be emotionally vulnerable to that person. While there are also mental and spiritual aspects to intimacy, it will suffice for now to define intimacy as emotional closeness

At times when I talk about both sexual intimacy and emotional intimacy, I mention them both. I want to add here that emotional intimacy and sexual chemistry sometimes feel inseparable, but for the sake of clarity, the times they feel separate demand that they be mentioned separately.

Chemistry: Chemistry is often used to describe sexual feelings and sexual attraction. Chemistry in the context of relationships is the interaction of one personality with another. There is nothing inherently sexual about personal chemistry. This book mentions several types of chemistry, including emotional chemistry, friendship chemistry (which I sometimes refer to as "depth of presence"), romantic chemistry, lifestyle chemistry or "lifestyle compatibility," and sexual chemistry. When I talk about sexual chemistry or romantic chemistry, I say exactly that.

Generally, the type of relationship that exists between two people will be determined by the chemistry present between those two people. This means that friendship chemistry will lead to a friendship; romantic chemistry will lead to a romantic relationship, and so on. Marriages do best when both people have sufficient relationship and communication skills and experience four types of chemistry between them: friendship chemistry, romantic chemistry, lifestyle chemistry, and wildly exciting sexual chemistry. I won't discuss all the different types of chemistry, but I will teach you how to respond to the chemistry you feel when you are with someone, whatever it is that you feel.

Skill: For the purposes of this book, skill is defined as a special ability often acquired by training. Like all skills, relationship skills must be learned by their rudimentary parts and then practiced and practiced and practiced until they feel natural. Let me give you a good illustration.

When I was 11 years old, I took my father's 8-iron into the yard with a couple of whiffle golf balls. I thought that if I did what felt "strong," then I would hit the ball far. But my "strong" way usually produced poor results. I hardly hit the ball at all, and I certainly didn't hit it well swinging the way I wanted to.

My father gently and patiently coached me so I could make a smooth, easy swing. It felt horrible, stiff, and restrictive. I hated doing it that way. Yet it worked. The ball flew high, straight, and far! What produced good golf shots consistently was doing it my dad's way. So I practiced it that way over and over and over.

So often, when I ask clients to try something new in their relationships, they say, "I'm not feeling it," or "that's not working for me." Of course it's not working for them! What "works" for them is doing the same old thing that led them to having bad, frustrating relationships in the first place! What feels "comfortable" to them produces poor results.

We have to step outside our comfort zone and try something new in spite of the awkwardness—and then practice, practice, practice, practice. When I talk about relationship skills and communication skills, I am talking about achieving a level of proficiency with doing the things that make relationships work well and recognizing and avoiding the pitfalls. Great relationships are a *learnable skill!* Awesome relationships require knowledge, awareness, and practice—*lots* of good practice.

God: In our modern age, we use several different words to describe a higher power. Some of these terms are Source, Spirit (or Great Spirit), Universe, Universal Intelligence, Vishnu, Creation, God, Elohim, Allah, and many more. All of these terms are speaking to an intelligence or design that is more powerful than we are. The word "God" in parts of the American culture has connotations of organized religion. Some people have serious differences with and wounds from organized religion and still feel deep faith in a higher power and Divine presence. For many such people, this has led to an aversion to using the word "God." In this book, I will not discuss or debate these differences; rather I will honor them all and focus on the spiritual aspects of relationships.

Shortly after I found my spiritual path, I was at an international gathering for world peace in Australia, where I heard a Native American elder named Joseph Rael speak. (Grandpa Joseph, as I call him, is the artist who painted the image on the back cover of this book.) Although English was not his first language, I expected him to use the word "Spirit," short for "Great Spirit," when he talked about a higher power. But he simply used the word "God." It impressed upon me that whatever we call our higher power, it is the higher power to which we are referring. (This is also reflected in the declaration of Islam, "There is no God but God.")

This book teaches the ways of relating to each other that lead to great relationships. They *are* based in a spiritual philosophy. This philosophy is not rooted in any one religion and is consistent with all religions. All human beings respond to each other in similar ways. Great relationships follow spiritual laws. The spiritual laws of relationships this book presents are not necessarily taught in churches, synagogues, ashrams, temples, and kivas; yet these teachings are conducive to the teachings shared in all these places. For purposes of brevity and flow, I simply use the word "God" to refer to all manner of higher power. I encourage each of you, as you read, to reinforce your own beliefs in Source, Higher Power, Spirit, Great Spirit, God, Vishnu, Elohim, Allah, or whatever name resonates with you as you read the word "God."

How This Book Is Organized

This book has two parts. Part One is called *The Four Pillars of Awesome Relationships* and it outlines the four main principles, which I call the four pillars, that create the mindset necessary to keep growing in a really good direction. If you do not get anything else out of this book, get the four pillars! Learn them. Remember them. See them operating in your life, and your relationships will explode with passion and closeness! The four pillars are:

1. It's Not About Joy or Pain, but Intensity.
2. Bright Lights Cast Dark Shadows.
3. Uncomfortable Feelings Are Like Rowdy Teenagers.
4. Love Is Not About Your Beloved—Love Is Feeling the Heart of God.

These pillars form the foundation of all the concepts in this book. These first four chapters outline the attitudes and beliefs necessary to heal buried hurts, use relationship conflicts as chances to get closer, and make relationships a path to God.

Part Two is called *The 12 Most Common Pitfalls of Relationships.* The 12 chapters in this section cover issues that are pervasive in your life and in the lives of everyone you meet. While keeping in mind the four pillars, you must also expand your awareness to include these 12 teachings in order to steer clear of the most serious potential problems in relationships. Learning to avoid these common pitfalls will ensure that your relationships not only become awesome, but stay that way indefinitely.

PART ONE:

THE FOUR PILLARS OF AWESOME RELATIONSHIPS

Chapter 1

It's Not About Joy or Pain, but Intensity

We all have a level of comfort with our emotions. This level acts as a type of thermostat to keep us "comfortable." Just as the thermostat in your house controls how hot or cold it feels in your home, your internal emotional thermostat controls the range of intensity that you are comfortable feeling.

We all want a maximum amount of joy in our lives, and we all want a minimal amount of pain. Who wouldn't want to feel massive joy and negligible pain? Unfortunately, that's not the choice that we actually get to make. The choice we get to make is about the intensity of our feelings— of *all* of our feelings. We get to decide how high we experience the highs, which is then directly related to how low we experience the lows. People never put a damper on their feelings to avoid more intense joy— only to avoid pain. But both are affected nonetheless. It's unavoidable.

The following two stories are good examples of this. The first tells how my friend Gloria began to awaken and heal as a result of falling in love. She came over one afternoon after a new relationship had just taken a big step forward in genuineness, excitement, authenticity, vulnerability, and especially closeness. She was acting a little hyper, almost short of breath, and her skin was glowing. She was visibly shaking, and she couldn't stop grinning.

"I don't know what to do," she said excitedly. "It's like, I like him— and my heart...." she broke off, hitting herself in the chest. "I can feel my heart! I can *feel* it! What the hell is *that?* I have never felt like this before!"

Then, with a look of amazement, she added, "I am scared to death!" I smiled, truly happy for her.

Gloria went on to compare how she felt in her previous relationship to how she was feeling in the present moment. "I always knew that Tim [her previous boyfriend] loved me, I never doubted that. But now—now I feel like I am going fly off into space at any moment because so much is going on inside." That's the way love is; it is incredibly exciting and incredibly scary at the same time. Our ability to feel these two seemingly different, opposite emotions (excitement and fear) is what determines our ability to experience all of what it means to truly be in love.

The second story illustrates the tragedy of a broken heart that never dared to love again. Jeffrey came into therapy with Cindy, his girlfriend of four years. The two of them sat in my office barely talking, and not sharing much when they did talk. Mostly, they looked like the life had been sucked out of them. Although they sat very close together on the couch, when they first arrived, I sensed no connection between them. They looked as if they were two strangers sitting on a bench together waiting for a bus.

After the first 15 minutes, therapy was going nowhere and I was getting bored. *Just imagine how they must be feeling after four years together if I am bored with them after 15 minutes*, I thought to myself. I don't usually ask about sex until a couple has attended at least two or three sessions. This couple in particular seemed to hold themselves so tightly that I thought they might both explode if they had to talk openly about sex. But I took a chance and asked anyway. I am glad I did, because they both perked up.

I saw a sparkle in their eyes and they began to act as if they were having fun together, talking freely about how exciting and passionate their relationship was in the beginning. Now that I could see the spark between them, my boredom dissipated, but I still didn't understand the lifelessness. I didn't know what had caused this couple to lose their passion and their excitement for each other (except sexually).

After some emotional investigation, Jeffrey admitted that he was still feeling the sting of a broken heart from a divorce. Although the human heart is not naturally shut down, people will shut their hearts whenever they do not want or feel able to handle the pain that they have buried inside.

Jeffrey had married his high school sweetheart. Following the dictums of his church, he waited until he and his bride were married before having sex. Jeffrey thought he was in the perfect marriage.

But slowly and steadily, he began to feel his wife shutting down both emotionally and sexually. The distance between them grew at a pace that was barely noticeable, but that covered quite a bit of territory over ten years of marriage. The effects were devastating. Jeffrey reported that his longing to be close to his wife never let up during their marriage, which just made the growing distance harder.

"It would have gotten so much easier over the last four or five years if I had just quit being attracted to her and quit caring," he said. "But I didn't." Love and passion became associated with pain, so he shut the love and passion off so he wouldn't have to feel his pain.

I reframed his statement with a bit of sarcasm. "It sounds like being in love with your wife is what made the relationship unbearable," I offered. "Loving her and loving making love with her kind of ruined the whole thing, didn't it?" He lit up and laughed for only an instant before returning to his drab, lifeless demeanor. Jeffrey had shut his heart down in order to *not* feel the daily anguish of losing his wife. His wife did not die; she just took herself away from him slowly.

Over the last four or five years of his marriage, the only time he would allow himself to feel his desire to be close to his wife was when he would consider leaving her. Then he would wake his heart back up, feel his love for her, feel the crushing pain of not being close to her, and muster up enough hope to "try harder" to make it work. Yet as hard as he tried, and in as many different ways as he tried, he felt defeated and hopeless.

His marriage eventually ended because he had an affair with Cindy, who had been in an equally sexless and passionless marriage. By the time Jeffrey met Cindy, she was a welcome escape from his marriage and he was just as much of a relief to her. When they got together, they were both amazed and delighted to have someone who responded with excitement and passion. For a while, they reveled in each other's exuberant love. They both got divorced, continued to date each other exclusively, and wanted to get married. Unfortunately, something stopped Jeffrey from getting closer as the relationship continued. He began to consistently cancel dates and miss appointments with Cindy.

The passion they shared was a great place to start in building a life together, and the joy they felt in the relationship created a strong bond. We will discuss in Chapter 2 how attraction can inspire us to heal old hurts and open to an intensity of joy we have not previously known. Jeffrey, however, was not healing. He refused to feel the intense buried hurt from his marriage. This prevented him from being able to open to the deeper emotional intimacy that was possible once he and Cindy were both available for a full relationship.

In order to turn the intensity meter on his feelings back up, Jeffrey needed to play catch up and feel the feelings that he had refused to feel before. When we don't feel buried feelings, they begin to call for attention and they disrupt our lives.

Jeffrey's unhealed and unfelt pain came out as his making excuses for not showing up for appointments and cancelling dates with Cindy. After four years, Cindy had still never met his children. His consistent failure to attend functions with her had gotten so bad that she was afraid to tell her family that she was coming into therapy with him. Her family was frustrated with Jeffrey and had been letting Cindy know that she deserved better than a man who refused to step up and show up. Jeffrey eventually quit coming into therapy once it became clear to him that to get anywhere, he would have to allow himself to feel more intense feelings.

Choosing to Shut Your Heart

Why would anyone choose to live with his or her heart shut down? When our emotional thermostat is set to a low intensity of feeling, we experience a low intensity of joy and a low intensity of pain. So with a shut-down heart, you are safe from the turmoil of hurting. As an added bonus, the shut-down heart wears blinders that keep it from seeing that it is shut down. Ignorance is bliss, right?

This type of ignorance, often called denial, is a very effective short-term coping tool. Denial can help us get through a hard situation. Similar to the fight-or-flight syndrome, denial can help us get by until we can find a place that feels emotionally safe. If we were in a real fight-or-flight situation (such as being chased by a tiger), a massive physical effort (such as running away or fighting back) would burn off all of the adrenaline and stress hormones our bodies would produce, and those stress hormones wouldn't become toxic. In an emotionally intense situation, we seek the same safety, and once we find it, we then need to work through the emotional trauma by feeling those hurt feelings so they do not become emotional toxins. In Chapter 3, we will discuss how to work through emotional traumas so they do not become emotionally toxic.

When I am speaking to a live audience, I use a play on words to describe the physical exercise needed to burn off stress hormones from our bodies as a metaphor for the emotional exercise we need to do in order to keep hurt feelings from turning into personal "demons" that need to be "exorcised." What I'm describing here is eliminating the pain from our physical and emotional chemistry. This doesn't mean ignoring the pain. To eliminate it, we must feel it so that the feelings can run their course, allowing the hurts to be truly resolved. Emotional pain, especially emotional trauma, will stay with us forever unless we heal the hurt. When we don't heal, we feel we have to shut down to a degree, because living with emotional pain is not sustainable.

That's why when we use denial as a long-term strategy, we pay for it with a part of our soul. The part of us that is hurt is no longer available to us or to the world. If it were *only* the hurt part of our hearts that shut down, we might be able to live pretty well, but that's not the way it works. First, *what we resist persists*. The hurt parts keep causing problems until they are healed (as we will see in Chapter 3). And second, *hiding the pain not only secludes the hurt part, it also takes every genuine feeling of equal or greater intensity and shuts it down also,* so as we lose the pain, we also lose the joy.

We must *take* the time and *make* the time to heal. Just as living with hurt is not sustainable, neither is living well without the full range of emotional intensity.

It is impossible to feel the immensity of love without an open heart. The problem is that we are not always aware that we've shut down our hearts. If we want to cultivate more emotional closeness in our lives, then we have to feel the excited state that is *intimacy*. And we can't feel any excited state with a shut-down heart. The task becomes finding a way to heal our old, buried hurts so we can begin to raise our level of emotional intensity. Then we can begin to comfortably handle greater levels of emotional excited-ness.

People often resist the idea of feeling hurts they've buried. They ask me, "Why would I want to feel that hurt?"

"Two reasons," I answer. "One, because that hurt carries with it an intensity of feeling, and when you feel something that intensely, then you also get to feel the intensity of joy that you want in your life. Two, when you feel the pain, that pain has a chance to run its course and grow into something else than can enrich your life. When that pain matures, you get to feel a gift where there used to only be hurt."

We don't normally think of pain as an excited state, but in order to heal we must begin to see the value in feeling our pain. In Chapter 3, we will learn the value of feeling pain and all of our uncomfortable feelings. For now, it's enough to understand that our feelings are not on a spectrum with joy on one side and pain on the other, where one is desirable and the other is not. Instead, feelings happen in degrees of intensity. Our ability to love in massive quantities and with massive quality comes with our ability to feel, and not run away from, our painfully intense emotions.

Wouldn't it be awesome to know that every feeling you have and every thought you think are for your highest good, aligned with your true spiritual nature? If you walk around defensively protecting the hurts that are buried inside, then those protected places are not open to the presence of God. If you are closed down, you can be present only to your own stories that support you staying shut down. Relationships are meant to bring up what you think you can't handle so that you can grow into being the kind of person who can handle everything that life has to throw at you. Relationships are meant to be a safe place to heal the hurts that get evoked. Learning and practicing the emotional and communication skills in this book will enable you to heal the hurts that have held you back and will give you the support to become the person you were meant to be and have the kind of relationship you were meant to have.

WHY WE SHUT DOWN

The reason we shut down begins with the pain we felt in our childhoods. As children, we did not have the emotional and cognitive resources to deal with those pains, so we shut down as a way to adapt. Shutting down becomes a habit. It's not natural, but it is the way human beings work in this world. We can't change that we got hurt, but we *can* heal so we can live fully from now on.

None of our parents did a perfect job of supporting us through our childhood hurts and emotional traumas. It may even have been our parents who caused a lot of those unpleasant experiences. We did not get the skills to be able to deal with hurts as they came, so we shut down a little. Can you imagine what childhood would have been like if, after being a jerk to you, one or both parents had apologized to you and talked about how to deal with their bad parenting so you would grow up emotionally healthy? The truth is that most of our parents didn't know how to deal with their *own* pain, much less have the perspective to be able to help us to deal with ours—especially when they were the ones who perpetrated the pain.

If the guidance we got from our parents didn't leave us equipped to handle pain and we wound up shutting down, then we also learn to develop thoughts (called adaptations) that keep us from being aware of the feelings that we shut down. Adaptations create detours in our thought patterns that protect us from feeling our hurts. They give us a way of maneuvering in the world so we aren't as likely to feel our pain, and they help us to remain ignorant of our pain on a daily basis.

Those adaptive thoughts do lead to feelings, but they're not the genuine feelings protected underneath. Adaptive thoughts are sort of like being in an emotional witness protection program. We end up feeling the feelings that go along with those adaptive thoughts (our "cover story"), and we act accordingly. Following that adaptive story line then deflects our attention and ensures that we avoid feeling our own hidden pain. We end up acting somewhat insincerely. It's not that we are intentionally being fake. It's more accurate to say that we are not being who we truly are.

If who we really are is a person who is hurt, then in order to be genuine, we need to feel that hurt and show (in an appropriate way) that we are feeling it. It's important to know that when I said earlier that feeling hurt is not sustainable, I was not suggesting that we need to walk around constantly feeling wounded. What I *am* saying is that we need to develop the skills to be able to heal our hurts instead of ignoring them, blaming them on others, and medicating them with anything that numbs us emotionally (be that drugs, alcohol, overeating, constantly being "too busy," or compulsively shopping on QVC).

If we remain aware of our hurts, then we can be more open to getting the support we truly need to heal. If we can begin to see how our thoughts, feelings, and behavior are based in deflecting pain (and thus how we avoid genuineness and authenticity), then we can get a clue about why our relationships don't satisfy our true needs and desires— it's because we aren't sharing our true needs and desires! All of this is done without our awareness; most of us get along pretty well in the world, so the emotional integrity police are not going to come out and start flogging us for avoiding our pain.

It is, however, important that when we are in pain, frustrated with a relationship, and feeling like we are at the end of our rope, we develop our awareness and begin filling the cracks and gaps in the emotional foundation of our relationships. When our hearts are closed this way, we have little chance of addressing our true needs in relationships. And if our true needs are not met in our relationships, we stand no chance of feeling healthy and fulfilled in those relationships.

Pain and Passion

Relationships are all about passion, fire, and excitement. That is the truest essence of two people coming together, and it is an incredibly exciting thing. We all feel excitement at the beginning of a relationship. In romance, we call it puppy love or infatuation. The feelings of infatuation are the same as falling in love—they inspire the same sensations that falling in love brings.

When we first meet someone, what we see in that person is about two percent reality and 98 percent fantasy. All we *really* know about the other person is what he or she looks like, how the other person carries himself or herself, what words he or she chooses to say, and how he or she sounds. Over time, we begin to see more and more of who the other person truly is and less and less of our fantasy about who that person is.

At some point, our awareness of our beloved becomes more reality than fantasy. That is when we often feel let down because the "glow period" is over. Couples come into my office complaining that their partner has changed. "What happened to the man I married?" they ask. "You're not the person I fell in love with," one will sometimes throw out at the other.

When that happens, I respond, "Of course this isn't the person you fell in love with! Who you fell in love with was your fantasy of your partner. In the beginning, the fantasy is always more powerful to us than the reality."

When I was discussing this with my wife, she said, "So I guess it is possible to fall in love for three months." She's right. The feelings we have in the beginning of the relationship are no less powerful, they are simply different than the feelings we will have in a longer-term relationship. As I often say, the excitement, infatuation, and feelings of love are real, but the person we think we are in love with is not—not entirely, anyway.

In light of this excitement, consider the emotional thermostat we talked about earlier. If we've shut down our intensity of feeling, then just like Jeffrey, we feel the excitement of a new relationship. Having a shut-down heart doesn't keep us from feeling the initial rush of infatuation; it only keeps us from being able to feel the intensity of our emotions as the relationship gets more real. While in the glow period, we don't feel shut down—we are opening, and it feels good. As we get closer, we have to continue to open up more to match the excitement and emotional intimacy we are cultivating. When the intimacy of the relationship calls us to feel genuine emotions more intensely than our thermostat allows, then we have to back away from going deeper in the relationship. This backing off from intimacy, while protecting us from feeling the hurts that come up, also prevents us from feeling a deeper sense of joy and closeness.

MAKING PEACE WITH THE PAIN

I have focused quite a bit on pain and how we must feel our pain. I do not mean to paint such a gloomy picture of relationships. But time and time again, I see people who have avoided feeling something they don't want to feel and have ended up miserable in relationships and frustrated in life. My goal for you is to feel massive amounts of joy! Joy is your birthright, and you deserve to be happy!

In order to be happy and maintain that happiness, you have to make peace with pain. As this chapter explains, pain is a fact of life. We will all be hurt at some point; we can't avoid it. When we develop the proper mindset and the emotional and communication skills we need to heal our hurts, we don't have to be afraid of or resistant to feeling our pain.

When we feel it, we begin to heal it. Leading a joyful life doesn't require us to go seek out pain, just to experience it when it happens. The more fully we feel our hurt, the more quickly it heals and the more free we are of our past and the more fully we get to feel our joy and pleasure when it comes in the next moment. By the time you get to the end of this book, you will have some skills to be able to handle pain with grace and get on to feeling the joy you deserve!

PRACTICES:

- Take one minute twice a day to dream of what you want your life and your relationship to be. Allow yourself to feel the excitement of your dreams. Do not allow any thoughts of "why the dream can't come true" to enter your mind during these two minutes each day. This is a time to feel your excitement and your passion—not your judgments.

- Make a list of two or three of your personal "don't go there" places—the biggest fears you have about yourself. Maybe you are scared of being a fraud or perhaps you feel guilty for something you did and the fear and the pain around this feels too great to share with anyone. These are the kinds of things that we don't even want to discuss with those closest to us because they might confirm our fear and we are not sure we could handle that. Look at your list and say to yourself, *These are the places where I refuse to grow. My fear is keeping me from finding out the truth about me.* Share your list with someone who is safe. Tell this person how scary it is to share these fears and admit that you may not be ready to confront the fear but that you want to begin the healing process by simply speaking aloud what the fears are.

- Next time you kiss and hug your partner, let yourself feel a little more excited than you normally do. Breathe your partner in as you kiss him or her. Feel your excitement more intensely, and savor the intensity of the experience for a few moments longer than you feel comfortable feeling it.

Chapter 2

Bright Lights Cast Dark Shadows

Love is the brightest light in the universe and we are all driven to love. The love we feel for each other and the love of God that shines through us as we love our beloved are some of the most evocative and compelling experiences we are capable of having.

When we feel attracted to another, in any way, we want to get closer to that person. The opening that occurs when we fall in love is the first part of a potential transformation. Love calls us to be vulnerable with our beloved. As we fall in love, it feels good to be vulnerable in the wonderful feelings of love. If we do not allow ourselves to be vulnerable, we stop the good feelings and we stop the transformational process. Why would anyone want to stop the awesome feelings that love brings? It doesn't seem logical, does it? Why would we keep ourselves from feeling one of the most wonderful feelings that human beings could feel? The answer lies in dark shadows.

Dark Shadows

As we get closer in a relationship, the bright light of love causes any unhealed hurt inside to show up as a very dark shadow. Those dark shadows *do not* feel good; we feel threatened, hurt, alienated, disrespected, resentful, scared, or unappreciated. These feelings do not feel like the wonderful love that has brought their darkness to light. When these feelings come up in the relationship, we have to feel them and share them with our beloved in order to heal them. When we allow ourselves to feel this hurt, and combine it with the opening that love brings, then love can begin to heal the hurt. This is why learning emotional, communication, and listening skills is so important in relationships! Without these skills, the hurts continue to pile up.

Usually the hurt will come up in one of two ways. Either the feelings of hurt, fear, disrespect, and so on will seem to come out of nowhere, or they will come out of a circumstance in the current relationship. When the feelings seem to come out of nowhere, this is the purest example of Bright Lights Cast Dark Shadows. Love evokes what needs to heal. In the case where hurt surfaces from some circumstances in the relationship, this is often an example of how destructive relationship patterns repeat themselves until the hurt is healed. In Chapter 3, we will discuss in detail how recurring themes and destructive cycles happen in our relationships. For now, it is enough to understand that recurring patterns in our life are love's way of trying to get our attention to heal the underlying hurt.

If we feel some kind of hurt in a relationship and avoid confronting the hurt, our avoidance will prevent us from getting closer to our beloved and it will prevent any resolution to the pain and ensuing conflict. In order to get closer, we have to begin to heal this hurt.

Avoiding pain is not a problem; unless you want to get closer to someone you love. When we want to get closer to someone and also want to avoid a buried pain, this is a perfect prescription for an "impasse." The father of Gestalt therapy, Fritz Perls, popularized the term "impasse," which he used to refer to the sick points in our lives and in our relationships. How many of us have ever come to an impasse in a relationship? Probably all of us!

When couples bump into these impasses or roadblocks and do not have the skills to heal the hurts and fears that come up, they get stuck. This stuckness is like putting one foot on the gas pedal of a car (wanting to feel the wonderful feelings of love) and simultaneously keeping a foot firmly on the brake pedal (avoiding feeling the deepest pain because of not knowing how to heal the issues that have come up). Couples then are stuck between feeling the love they have for each other and the inability to heal the hurts they feel. This is the point where most couples begin to fight.

FIGHTING

Couples fight to avoid feeling pain that is buried inside, but the problem is that fighting usually *causes* more pain. If we do not have the courage, faith, and especially the skills to feel and heal the hurt that is being uncovered by the love we have, we have no choice but to stop getting closer to each other. When we stop getting closer to each other, we stop the unresolved hurt inside from coming up. At the most basic level, couples fight because they want to get closer and at the same time they don't want to feel vulnerable.

I know what you're thinking: *Couples fight in an effort to get closer to each other? How could fighting bring us closer?* Yes, it's true that most couples fight as an effort to resolve the differences that keep them from getting close. I didn't say that fighting *gets* them closer. I said it was *an effort* to get closer. I am all for resolving the differences that keep us from getting closer to each other—that is what this whole book is about. It's just that fighting is a ridiculous way to try to get close to someone.

Usually in order to fight, you have to do four ridiculous things:

1. Ignore the feelings of love you have for the person in that moment. That's ridiculous!
2. Have the intention of winning the fight, not the intention of getting closer. That's really ridiculous!
3. See the other person's feelings as an impediment to your happiness. This is the same as not caring for the other person in that moment. That's incredibly ridiculous!
4. Not care how you speak to the other person. If you do not care how your words land with someone you love, you are a relationship idiot!

When I talk about fighting, I am not talking about having a logical debate. I love having logical debates because they help people to be clear about what they feel and believe. The problems come when someone loses focus on discovering the truth and tries to "win." Winning an argument is about protecting your ego and avoiding being emotionally vulnerable.

Most arguments are based on the principle that if I prove that I am right, or at least that you are not right, then I will win and the argument and the pain will be gone. This implies one of two things: either if I win (no matter how I win), we will get to be close again as soon as the argument is won, or that it doesn't matter how close we are after the argument. In essence, "You don't matter to me."

Both of these are faulty principles: In the first case, it is how we interact that determines how close we are, not whether we are right or wrong. We will discuss this more in Chapter 16. In the second case, if the person with whom you are arguing doesn't matter, you have no reason to be arguing—just walk away. This is what smart people do. The only reason to fight is to try and protect your ego by proving you are "right," or to avoid the necessary vulnerability involved in creating emotional intimacy. In relationships, the sole focus of a disagreement needs to be creating more emotional intimacy. People argue only because they do not have the relationship skills to be able to resolve the impasse they have come to in their relationship.

RELATIONSHIPS CALL US TO HEAL

This is an important point, so I am going to scream it at you. When we come to an impasse and begin to feel afraid, IT IS NOT YOUR BELOVED WHO IS SCARY TO YOU. IT IS THE FEELINGS THAT WILL COME UP INSIDE OF YOU IF YOU GET CLOSER TO YOUR BELOVED THAT ARE SCARY. YOUR SUBCONCIOUS MIND KNOWS YOU MIGHT FEEL BURIED PAIN, SO IT COMES UP WITH A VERY "REASONABLE" SOUNDING STORY TO KEEP YOU FROM DOING ANYTHING THAT MIGHT CAUSE YOU TO FEEL THE BURIED PAIN. The scared/conditioned mind will come up with *any* story it can to convince you that it is your beloved who is the source of your fear and/or pain. It is the job of the conditioned mind to keep you away from your buried hurt, so it tries to blame your beloved or the situation.

It seems easier to blame your beloved for your fear than it is to face the hurts that you have buried inside. I did not say it *is* easier to blame your beloved, I said it *seems* easier. When you consider the long-term effect on your life and the effects on your relationship, it certainly is not easier to blame your beloved for the uncomfortable feelings coming up inside. Over time, blame will take its toll on your happiness, joy, and intimacy. Instead, I challenge you to choose the greater task of acknowledging your own feelings, taking responsibility for them, and ceasing to deflect or project them onto your beloved. There is a risk involved in this practice—you risk feeling more love than you ever thought you could handle. I hope you are up for it!

Love brings the opportunity to heal. For people in awesome relationships, love inspires them to work through the issues that come up with their beloved. Relationships compel us to "show up" fully with our beloved. Whenever we have an unhealed hurt, which we all do, it keeps us from completely engaging in our relationships. A wounded heart is shut down to a degree. Love is the powerful enzyme that opens our hearts and creates the safety for us to become vulnerable. As we become vulnerable, our beloved is able to touch us more deeply.

The couples who come into my office invariably started off with an incredible connection with each other and were really in love. By the time they come in, they are feeling incredibly frustrated. What they are frustrated with is that they feel hurt and they don't have the skills to heal the hurt. When the hurts are healed, they get to enjoy their closeness and intimacy again.

Every couple that comes to me complains that they don't communicate or don't communicate well. While that is true, it is really more of an issue that they don't have the emotional and relationship skills, which include communication, to be able to heal the hurts and fears that keep coming up. About 40 percent of these couples are scared that the connection has been completely lost. The other 60 percent are just as miserable and their relationships are in just as much trouble; the only difference is that they know their connection is still there even though they don't get to enjoy it. Neither of these couples is any happier than the other.

I Give You All of Me

Remember Jeffrey, our case study in Chapter 1? Jeffrey began to fall in love with Cindy as his marriage was ending. He was excited in his new relationship and felt his heart come alive again. Jeffrey and Cindy happily kept getting closer, feeling the rapture of love. At some point the excitement that was drawing them closer came into conflict with Jeffrey's unresolved pain (and subsequent shut-down). The love and excitement Jeffrey felt for Cindy had brought him to the point where he needed to heal his old hurt in order to continue to build a closer relationship with Cindy. The light of love had drawn him closer to Cindy and it was that light that was providing the opportunity to heal.

In a relationship, we all want our entire partner. I want my wife to give herself to me entirely! I want to give all of myself to her. If there's some part of me that I'm not okay with, and that I'm not willing to feel (an old hurt), then that's a part of me that I am going to have to make peace with if I'm going to get closer to my wife. The closeness will continue to grow in a relationship until this barrier is reached. All relationships encounter this to some degree. It is the couples who have the relationship skills to be able to heal the hurts and resolve the internal and interpersonal conflicts who have the most awesome relationships.

Relationships as a Spiritual Practice

The path to God is through enlightenment. What keeps us from being enlightened is our own unresolved pain. We are enlightened to the degree to which we are *open* and free from emotional conflict. By paying attention to how we feel in relationships, we can notice when we are *closed down* or *closed off*.

When our awareness is open, we are susceptible to feeling any unhealed hurt we carry and we are also susceptible to feeling the love of our beloved, the love of family and friends, and the love of God. When we are closed in some way, the part of us that is not fully open is not receptive to *all* of what is available at each moment—including God's presence and the opportunity to feel God's blessing in an acute and personal way. So it is only when our awareness is fully open that we can become aware of the full effect of God's presence and God's love in our lives.

It is also true that intimacy is facilitated by openness and it is hindered by *being closed off*. With this perspective, it is easy to see how creating emotional intimacy does the same things necessary to create spiritual enlightenment. Relationships are the media in which we act out and experience most of our spirituality. Most of how we experience our spirituality is accomplished without our awareness of the spiritual significance of what is happening. Most of us are not aware of the spiritual significance of our daily interactions in our relationships. It is my personal belief that any spiritual path or religion that does not teach the emotional skills for healthy relationships is missing the most profound opportunity to teach its patrons to embody the spiritual truth it teaches.

HOLLOW BONE

Native American teachings often use the metaphor of the hollow bone. If you cut the ends off of an animal bone, you would see that it is full of marrow and nothing can get through. In the teaching of the hollow bone, the marrow is symbolic of our psychological conflict and unresolved pain. If you clean the bone out, you will see that it's hollow. If you get it clean enough, you will see that the inside of the bone is so smooth that it is shiny.

The metaphor teaches that we, as hollow bones, are conduits for God's love to come into this world. The more we clean out our emotional turmoil, the greater volume of God's love can come through us to do God's work in the world. This work is done through us in how we live our lives. God's work is either done or not done in how we treat each other and the decisions we make. It is only when we are undistracted by our own unresolved emotional needs that we can be of great service to the planet by embodying or being a conduit of God's love.

The cool thing is that we get to be the embodiment of God's love by being who we truly are! We don't have to change or be someone else; we just have to heal the hurts that lead us to be disingenuous. Our genuine nature is to love. It is only our unresolved pain that keeps us from loving and treating ourselves and others lovingly. Being closed off not only hurts our relationships in those moments, it also diminishes our ability to be the hollow bone that brings God's blessing and God's presence into our lives, into our partners' lives, and into the world.

How many times have you known people who love each other and start out feeling like God has blessed them by putting their beloved in their lives—only to end up so hurt, angry, and frustrated that they blame their beloved for their hurt? This dynamic prevents any further chance they have of feeling God's blessing through the presence of the other. If you want spiritual enlightenment and/or relationship success, you *must* incorporate emotional health and sound relationship skills into your spiritual awareness and acknowledge the spiritual awakening that is possible in all your relationships, especially your intimate relationships. In Chapter 4, we will discuss some specific practices for embodying love and being a loving presence in the world.

Do relationships serve a spiritual need or does our spiritual growth facilitate greater relationships? Both and neither: No separation exists between the two. The closer we want to get, the more we have to heal. The more we heal, the closer we get to each other and to God. Relationships need to serve as a practice on our spiritual path *and* at the same time our spiritual walk needs to support healthy emotional connections. How does this work?

PROCESS OF RELATING AS A SPIRITUAL PRACTICE

$$L > O > V > H > A = B$$

LOVE/ATTRACTION → OPENING → VULNERABILITY → HEALING → AUTHENTICITY = BLESSING

We start off feeling *love* and *attraction*. The feelings of love lead to us *opening* our hearts. When we begin to open, we have to either become *vulnerable* or stop getting closer. If we are willing to become vulnerable, we must *heal* the unresolved hurts that emerge from our opening, vulnerable heart. After healing, we are capable of being more *authentic*, more of who we truly are. More authenticity leads to our ability to feel God's *blessing* in our lives. The most common stumbling block to intimacy and spiritual blessing is vulnerability (more on this later).

What Are the Limits?

People often ask me if it is possible to be 100 percent open spiritually and 100 percent healed from all emotional pain. My answer is always a resounding *yes*, but that is not the real question they're asking. What people are *really* asking is, does their happiness have limits? There are no limits to happiness, enlightenment, and connection. Instead of believing in limits, we need to stay focused on opening when the opportunities for opening come, healing when the chances to heal come, and reveling in joy when moments of joy happen.

The most common question clients ask me is whether or not it is really possible to heal at all or if we are just destined to suffer the same woes forever. Hear this: *It is possible to heal. There is nothing from which you cannot heal.* We will probably always have a few scars; when the emotional hurt is gone, a scar just becomes a good story to tell. It is entirely possible to feel really, really good most of the time. We will all have good times and hard times, but when we heal and we live with strong, open hearts embracing who God truly meant for us to be, then the hard times aren't nearly as hard and are only seen as exciting new challenges.

I have said that when someone does become completely free, having healed *all* internal conflict and emotional pain in his or her life, and is completely open spiritually, that person would just turn into a dancing ball of light and no longer exist on this planet. Until that point when we all become these wonderfully enlightened bundles of light and energy, we are going to be in these human bodies and we're going to have these energetic and biochemical processes called feelings. So we need to live in such a way that our thoughts, feelings, and actions support us in creating the kind of lives we want and are capable of having. Understanding that the problems that come up in relationships are really opportunities to heal is a necessary first step in our transformation.

Problems Are Opportunities

When we shift our awareness from avoiding problems to embracing problems, our relationship conflicts become an adventure of intimate discovery. It is excruciating to know you are hurting and *not* to have the skills to be able to heal it. We all have a natural tendency to back away when we are scared. Transformational teacher T. Harv Eker defines fear as "anticipation of pain." We *back away* from something to avoid our anticipated pain when we are scared. This reaction was entirely adaptive in pre-historic times when early humans experienced physical threats on a semi-regular basis. But as we have seen, this is *not* an adaptive strategy for dealing with emotional pain. Of course, this is not to say that we don't need to set firm boundaries with someone who is causing us harm. (We will talk about boundaries in Chapter 7.)

Backing away from pain does not help us to heal, it does not help us to be close to one another, and it does not keep the door open for love and connection to transform our hurts. What we truly *desire* is to feel our love with our beloved. Backing away from our beloved when we are scared does not allow us to feel love. If we emotionally *back away* from our beloved, then we put a limit on the love, closeness, and joy that we can feel in that moment. The point of relationships is to bring us closer to each other and to God. We get closer to God when we *step in* closer to our beloved and to our hurt when problems come up because we are stepping deeper into ourselves and bringing more of who we truly are into the world.

Good News!

God wants us to feel joy. God wants us to have fun together. God wants us to heal. God wants each of us to know our own wonderfulness. In order to make sure we pay attention to the chance to do all this, God puts love and our beloved in our life. Knowledge, awareness, and willingness to take action are power. When you enter into a relationship armed with the knowledge and awareness contained in this book and you are courageously willing to do things differently and develop new habits, then miracles and magic will happen in your life.

Someone once defined magic for me as "paying attention to reality in ways that most people are accustomed to ignoring." This applies to relationships. If you begin to pay attention to your relationships in ways that most people ignore, then you will begin to see things that most people don't see; you will have seemingly "magical" relationship awareness. When you are aware of your own needs at the deepest levels, you will begin to see and support one another's growth and healing. As you begin to feel your own genuine emotions more deeply, you will begin to notice other people's emotions (including those they may not even be aware of), and these people will be amazed at how deeply you see into them. As you begin to heal, you become an agent of healing change in your family, in your community, and in the world.

The first step to making the world a better place is to heal your own relationships and begin to feel the love of God blessing you and your union with your beloved. Healing your own relationships is much easier when you recognize that Bright Lights Cast Dark Shadows. It is love itself that is bringing up the problems between you. Love is uncovering the problems in your relationships to show you what needs to heal for the two of you to approach enlightenment. The problems that come up in relationships are blessed feedback showing you the places in your life where you need to heal. Being open to this feedback, even during the painful parts, and giving thanks for the transformation that is possible is one of the secrets of turning relationships into sacred bliss.

PRACTICES:

- Think of hurt feelings as God saying, "This hurt is a place where you have not let me in." This helps you reframe the situation so that instead of seeing it as something painful that you understandably want to push away, you can begin to see it as an opportunity for something wonderful—getting closer to God and filling your life with more joy. In this view, you can see the hurt feelings as a *gift* and a *blessing*.

- Imagine your hurt as your beloved saying, "I don't want you to hurt and this is showing you a place where we can love each other more." Again, this helps you reframe what you are trying to avoid, allowing you to see it for the opportunity that it is.

- When you feel hurt in your relationship, say this prayer, *"God, thank you for blessing me with this love that shows me where I need to heal."* Then say to your beloved, "Thank you for coming into my life. You have loved me well enough for this hurt to come up and now it is time for me to heal it."

- Think of five or six times when you thought your relationship was going pretty well until you suddenly felt blindsided by someone's anger or judgment, and then felt as though you were being shamed or pushed away. Consider if the real issue may have been the other person's fear of letting you get too close and having to deal with his or her own insecurities about that. Remember that being aware of this dynamic is vital to maintaining your emotional center when someone else gets triggered.

CHAPTER 3

HURT FEELINGS ARE LIKE ROWDY TEENAGERS

When I was building a swing set fort for my kids, I got a mondo-splinter in my left middle finger. I got most of it out immediately and thought it was all gone. The bleeding soon stopped, and I never quit working. It still hurt slightly for a couple of days, so I avoided using it in a way that would agitate the pain. After a week, I had a slight callous on my finger that I noticed only when I pressed on something. *It shouldn't be hurting*, I thought. *That happened a week ago*. But I continued to ignore it.

After another few weeks, it still hurt when I squeezed something really hard or when I bumped my finger against something. I realized that I still had a tiny piece of wood in my finger. Wouldn't it be great if ignoring a problem made it go away? The pain always went away quickly, so I didn't do anything about it. But I did notice that I used the other hand for some things that I usually did with my left hand. After a while, my finger got infected and began to abscess. The abscess felt like a painful bubble of pressure as it continued to grow, although it never managed to push the piece of splinter out. It would flare up, and then go away; flare up again, then go away again. And each time it would go away, I would forget about it.

As you can imagine, after the third or fourth time my finger got inflamed, I knew that I needed to do something about it. So I dug the rest of the splinter out. I had to cut through the callous, cut through healthy tissue, and relieve the pressure. I had to cut, tear, and squeeze at the wound. My wife said that my face had gone white; it hurt like hell!

But despite the pain, I removed the remnant of the splinter. I packed the wound with goldenseal and grape seed extract and wrapped it up. Guess what happened next? It *healed!*

To this day, I haven't noticed it again and wouldn't know I ever had a wound there except when I look at it to tell the story. There is *no* pain at all, and I can use my left hand normally. If I had continued to ignore the problem, I would probably continue to have periodic abscesses, the embedded splinter would have continued to hurt when it got bumped, and I would still be unconsciously avoiding using my left hand in certain ways—using an adaptation to deal the pain. As we saw from Chapter 1, we form adaptations to help us steer clear of feeling the feelings we want to avoid. I wanted to avoid the pain of squeezing something with my finger so I used my other hand at times. Adaptations keep us from doing what might otherwise be a natural action, either physically or emotionally.

In this case, the embedded splinter is a metaphor for any buried hurt that keeps us from feeling love, treating others lovingly, receiving love, setting appropriate boundaries, knowing our own wonderfulness, or living excited and passionate lives. Our buried pain and unresolved hurts are the metaphorical embedded splinters that keep us from living the lives we dream about. It hurts to bump an embedded splinter, so we try to avoid the pain. Most of us deal with our emotional wounds in relationships this same way; we try to avoid "bumping" the hurt places. Unhealed physical wounds keep causing problems, like the abscesses in my finger, until they are given a real chance to heal. Unhealed emotional wounds keep getting our attention in the most annoying ways until we give them the attention they need to heal.

ROWDY TEENAGERS

Unhealed buried hurts are like *rowdy teenagers!* When rowdy teenagers are acting up, we just want them to shut up and go away! Well, teenagers don't actually need to go away; what they need is to *mature*. The way uncomfortable feelings mature is by feeling them. When you finally feel the hurt that you have avoided feeling, that hurt can begin to heal.

What happened to Abby is a perfect example. Abby was violently mugged in Chicago in the mid-'70s. She was absolutely horrified and terrorized by the experience. She thought she was going to be raped and killed. She never dealt with the emotional trauma afterward. She never dealt with the fear. Instead, she ignored the pain and fear. *I am a strong woman*, Abby said to herself. *I will be just fine.*

When we have a wound, it will keep sneaking out subconsciously to get our attention, just like a rowdy teenager who won't be quiet or go away. Since the original terrorizing mugging in the '70s, Abby was mugged every four or five years, in every city where she has ever lived. Subconsciously, she continued to put herself in dangerous situations over and over and over again. By refusing to accept and heal the feelings from her original mugging and continuing to insist to herself, *I will be fine*, Abby subconsciously ignored legitimate safety concerns in her daily life.

At the end of every therapy session, she acted flustered when it came time to pay me; she would pull out a large wad of bills and shuffle through them, handing me bills haphazardly. This is the way Abby paid her tab at bars, too, she admitted later. Then she would leave the bar late at night by herself, refusing to let anyone walk her to her car, again insisting to herself, *I am a strong woman—I will be fine*. She also refused to spend time with men who treated her well and described men who spoke respectfully to her as "soft," preferring what she termed "real" men. This preference usually relegated her to a pretty rough crowd of people who treated her badly. Her spirit was calling her to heal that original hurt, and she refused to do it. She felt too scared to look at the pain, too scared to look at the terror that she experienced. Because she refused to heal the emotional trauma, she continued to receive tragic reminders that she needed to heal.

The human heart will not tolerate being shut down forever. Instead, it will periodically remind us of our buried hurts. It is annoying to get these reminders, just like rowdy teenagers are annoying. These reminders keep coming up to give us the choice to heal the underlying hurt or continue to suffer the consequences. The consequences of healing are *so* much better than the consequences of *not* healing!

ADAPTATIONS

When you feel an uncomfortable feeling, chances are your mind will say to you, *Stop this pain. It is never going to end. I can't handle this!* But your mind is telling you a big, fat lie! We develop habits that keep us from bumping the "embedded splinters" of our hearts, just like how I quit using the middle finger on my left hand to avoid feeling the hurt it would cause. These habits are like detours that we take around what would naturally be a topic, feeling, or person we may run into.

A client named Shelly once described one of her adaptations that was quite literally a detour. Shelly had grown up with an abusive mother. Whenever she saw her mother, she would become so anxious and panicked that she would begin to feel trapped. As time went on, she started feeling anxious when she drove past her mother's business, scared she would see her mother as she drove by. Shelly began taking a longer route to work, adding five minutes to her daily commute, so she didn't have to drive past her mother's business. She avoided going to the bank after seeing her mother in line to make a deposit. Eventually, Shelly began to feel nervous about going anywhere in her car, scared she might see her mother.

When Shelly initially came to see me, she had a great deal of emotional awareness. She knew what she was feeling and what was triggering her feelings. But she didn't know *why* she was getting so triggered or how to heal the hurt that was being triggered. She was confused about why her symptoms were not going away and why they had gotten more intense over the last three years. Previous therapy and a earning a degree in social work had helped her to develop the emotional awareness, but she still carried all the emotional trauma and related adaptations. I explained that God has a way of sometimes turning up the heat on us.

"When we need to heal," I explained to Shelly, "God doesn't want us to suffer, so she does the most compassionate thing she can—she puts a flame under our denying butts! God wants to make sure we get the message to heal the hurts we keep running away from. When we neglect a part of us, that part will continue to make stronger and stronger attempts to get the attention it needs. This is the same reason most addicts will get deeper and deeper into their addiction, with more and more denial, until they finally hit rock bottom."

After several months of therapy, another client named Rachel began noticing that she consistently avoided making eye contact with men she was genuinely attracted to and consistently went on dates with men who didn't really interest her. She began to realize that this lifelong pattern had always served to keep her from facing her feelings of worthlessness. By dating men to whom she was not attracted, she never felt the passion that would have challenged her feelings of low self-worth. The problem seemed to get worse because she got increasingly frustrated that the guys she was dating seemed to be become more and more dull.

During one session, she described what she felt when she made eye contact with a man to whom she *was* attracted who was also attracted to her. "If I let *that* guy close to me," she said, "then I am gonna feel a hundred feet tall and I am going to have to believe in myself and that I deserve that kind of excitement. So instead I looked away and avoided him. I wound up going to tea with a *dufus* who bored me outta my mind!" Her habit of avoiding eye contact with men she was attracted to was an adaptation that allowed her to never confront her pain around worthiness.

The impact these adaptations have on our relationships is not worth the effort. *Effort?* I know you are asking. *I am not aware of putting forth any effort to hide my pain.* Of course you aren't! Part of the function of an adaptation is to cover its own tracks. Adaptations not only try to hide the hurt, but they also try to hide the fact that anything is hidden. A really effective adaptation will enable you to quickly forget that you ever had a hurt that you wanted to avoid.

Imagine if the energy involved in hiding your hurts and hiding the fact that you are hiding your hurts was directed to generating closeness and intimacy and getting the support you need to heal. It would be like adding racing fuel to your car's engine! Suddenly, the things that felt too hard might seem possible—not easy, but possible.

THE PRICE WE PAY

When a problem comes up in a relationship, it *seems* easier to avoid the problem by blaming our partner, ignoring the situation, ignoring each other's hurt, finding a new relationship, or just hoping it gets better on its own. While it *seems* easier in the short-term to avoid the problem in these ways, the long-term effects are devastating. This type of avoidance will slowly degrade the quality and depth of our emotional contact and communication. We make decisions a thousand times a day that either get us closer to each other or keep us away. Adaptations guide us to make decisions that are ultimately self-defeating, because our decisions, while keeping us from facing a fear, will be based on ignoring an important part of who we are. And that, in turn, keeps us from getting closer and creating more intimacy in our lives.

So we have these feelings we don't like, and we bury them deep inside. Ignoring those feelings keeps us from being fully present with each other, because it is impossible to be emotionally close without being emotionally present. In a further effort to avoid feeling our buried pain, when a hidden hurt gets bumped, most of us get mad at our partner or feel hurt that the relationship doesn't feel good. Well, of course the relationship doesn't feel good! When we ignore a part of our heart, and push our beloved away to further avoid that part of our heart, we are refusing to do what it takes to make the relationship feel good. By taking adaptive detours away from our hurts, we are cutting off the chance for deeper intimacy—even though deeper intimacy is what we want with our partner in the first place!

We have all seen someone who tries to hide a hurt by avoiding and denying. Some people do it quite well—until the hiding gets in the way of normal healthy function. And *true* normal healthy function means no less than feeling like and being the embodiment of love. At some point, I hope we all dig out the splinters that are the source of our emotional wounds and allow those wounds to fully heal rather than to keep taking detours around them.

PREPARING FOR THE INEVITABLE

Each time we come into contact with our beloved, we have the opportunity for one of our emotional "embedded splinters" to get bumped. We will get hurt, feel attacked, get disappointed, and so on. It is going to happen! A natural and wonderful pull brings us closer when the chemistry is just right. That chemistry pulling us closer means we *will* have our old emotional wounds "bumped." Awesome relationships are not the relationship where we don't bump each other's emotional hurts. They are the ones where both people know that their wounds are going to come up and they have the strategies and skills to handle the inevitable conflicts—and even use those conflicts to heal *with* each other and grow closer as a result.

ROWDY TEENAGERS GROW UP/GIFTS OF EMOTIONAL MATURITY

When rowdy teenagers mature into adults, they bring their natural-born gifts to society. If a rowdy teenager *never* matures, then he or she *never* brings those God-gifted talents to the world. Likewise, when we heal the hurts that are buried inside, we give ourselves the gift of getting a wonderful part of ourselves back. If we go our entire lives without ever healing a particular hurt, the exciting and excited part of us that is buried underneath that pain will stay buried forever.

When an uncomfortable feeling matures, it brings an excited, vibrant piece of who we are back into our lives. Healing returns to us the part of ourselves that got buried with the hurt. As you remember from Chapter 1, healing a hurt brings back a level of intensity and passion that was previously hidden. In addition to feeling more whole, we get the ability to be more present and more authentic in our relationships, which ultimately opens the door to walking a more authentic spiritual path.

I often use the phrase, "You have to feel it to heal it." When the pain begins to emerge, it is coming up to be felt. We have to "stay with the pain," which means we need to keep feeling it and *not* run away from it. When we stay with the pain and continue to feel it, it can heal. And then the pain doesn't hurt anymore.

I liken the healing of emotional pain to the physical pain one feels in athletic training. Competitive cyclists have a saying: The winner is the guy with the best relationship to pain. As a bicycle racer myself, I've discovered that when I'm riding a bike so hard that my legs begin to hurt, I have three choices: I can back off the effort, I can maintain the same intensity, or I can push even harder. If I maintain the same intensity or push harder, I am going to continue to feel pain, but I will also create an awesome opportunity! After a painful effort, with proper rest, my legs come back stronger, with more endurance; the same amount of physical work will not hurt like it did before. In essence, by hurting and then resting, I can increase my capacity to handle faster bicycle riding.

Athletes know that pain in training is the key to greater performance on game day. It is the same with emotional pain. Most of us were never taught that the ability to feel our emotional pain is the key to greater intimacy, not to mention more emotional safety, security, love, trust, self-worth, and ultimately success in life. Just as an athlete has no greater satisfaction than reaching peak performance, a couple experiences no greater payoff than feeling deep, exciting, and lasting intimacy in their relationship.

Competitive cyclist Lance Armstrong once explained: "Pain is temporary. It may last a minute, or an hour, or a day, or a year, but eventually it will subside and something else will take its place. If I quit, however, it lasts forever." Whether you read that as physical pain or emotional pain, the quote conveys the kind of confidence and fearlessness that teaches us not to be afraid of our pain. When we apply this principle of staying with our emotional pain, knowing it will eventually subside, we can be comforted in the fact that although the pain *feels* like it will never end, the pain will indeed subside. When we heal an emotional pain, a greater presence, love, and joy replaces it.

A month or so after my son was born, my wife went out to lunch with our midwife. The midwife asked, "You labored for 31 hours, and you pushed for 5 hours, but you never complained or said, 'I can't do this.' I have never seen any woman do that before. How did you do that?"

My wife, a bona fide goddess, responded, "I knew that eventually it was going to be over. Fighting against it wouldn't make it hurt less. I was either going to have a kid or I was going to die. Either way, it was going to end." My wife trusted that her body had the skills to have a baby and that everything would be okay, even when she didn't know how that was going to happen. She breathed into the pain and never resisted it. What a bad ass! I am thankful to have her.

GOOD COACHING

In sports, it's very easy to see when somebody is not putting in the work. All good athletes have really good coaches to guide them and hold them accountable for putting forth the necessary effort. In relationships, it is much harder to see when we are not doing the work because we *all* come up with stories that justify our perspective. It feels easier and safer to blame our partner rather than accept responsibility for our own uncomfortable feelings. It feels easier to justify than to feel vulnerable. Again, it isn't easier in the long run—it only seems that way short term.

Having a good relationship coach can offer guidance by pointing out all the places where we are blinded by our own stories. On our own, most of us haven't developed the awareness needed to turn emotional upsets and frustrations into deeper emotional intimacy. I encourage everyone to attend one of my workshops, find a good therapist, or work with a relationship coach.

The bottom line is that we can't avoid our pain forever. Buried pain will not be denied its voice. The sooner we begin to heal it, the sooner we begin to enjoy our lives more than ever before. Whenever we feel hurt, disappointed, or attacked, we can choose to celebrate the chance to heal the wound we have just uncovered.

PRACTICES:

- If you consistently feel upset or disappointed by something that is happening in your life or you feel as though no matter how hard you try you just can't win or you just can't get ahead, it is not your external circumstances that are holding you back. Even if you do not understand how you are creating or helping to contribute to the problem, say to yourself, *I am creating this, over and over in my life. Even though I don't like it or understand it, I am going to become aware of my part in it and heal the hurts that are getting in the way of me getting what I want.*

- When you recognize one of these hurtful or disappointing patterns in your life, say to yourself, *Thank you, God! Thank you for showing me again and again what I need to heal. I am ready to look at it now!* Then take a deep breath and feel the hurt and know the pain will not kill you, it will only *seem* as though it will.

- Take a few minutes to journal about a recurring pattern in your life that feels frustrating. Ask yourself, *What lesson is this pattern here to teach me?* If your answer feels defeating, that's not the right answer. If your answer inspires you, you are on the right track. Pick someone to support you and share your findings.

- When you are faced with tough situations over and over, ask yourself, *What qualities would I have to have to handle this with grace?* Then take a moment to realize that those are the qualities and gifts that are buried underneath the hurt that drives this recurring problem, and imagine what it would feel like to feel fully empowered by them. When you heal the hurt, you get the gifts!

CHAPTER 4

LOVE IS NOT ABOUT YOUR BELOVED— LOVE IS FEELING THE HEART OF GOD

If you had to choose between an ever-flowing love that illuminates every aspect of your life or a love that sets you up for potential heartbreak and soul-crushing loss, which would you choose? Pretty simple choice, huh? How about choosing between a love based in deep connection, fun, and acceptance or a love that threatens judgment, abandonment, and drama? Still easy, right? Now consider these questions:

- Do you feel as though you give more love than you receive?
- Do you wish you could get your partner to give you the love and attention you want?
- Are you scared of losing the love you already have?
- Are you "in love" and hate the way your partner talks to you/ treats you?
- Are you an embodiment of love in the world?

If you do not feel like a wellspring of love, continuously renewed, constantly showered in love, and constantly showering your partner in love, then you need this chapter!

We have a choice about how we love, and we make this choice every second of the day. Most of us are not aware that we have this choice— we are not aware of how we love, the true source of love, or what love means. But our choices and our beliefs about love have a dramatic effect on how we treat and respond to those we love, whether we realize that or not.

The bottom line is that you can change how you love and how much you love right now! You can change the love you receive right now! You can infuse your current relationship with a thrilling, illuminating love or attract a new relationship where you feel love bursting forth between you at all times.

First, however, I want you to be very clear on where love comes from and where love does *not* come from. You may believe that the source of love is your beloved. It seems fairly clear, doesn't it? You didn't feel love until you came into contact with your beloved; therefore it must be your beloved who brings the love to you. Maybe you felt empty until your beloved came into your life, then you felt full. Maybe you were bored and began feeling excitement when your beloved showed up. No matter what the situation, feeling wrapped up in love with another person *must* mean that the love is coming from the other person, right? In reality, it's not even close.

To understand the true source of love, imagine a cylinder of light coming down from above, like you see in movies under the center of a spaceship. Imagine that cylinder is a beam of pure love coming directly from the heart of God. Now imagine someone to whom you are greatly attracted standing on the other side of that cylinder. The cylinder of love keeps sending out little lightning bolts that excite you and pull you closer to each other. You see that the other person is just as excited as you are, and seeing the other person's excitement makes that person even more alluring. You feel your desire, and with every quickening breath you can't tell a difference between your heart and your head; both are saying, *yes!* Finally, driven by your own desire to get closer to this other person, you step into the cylinder of light. The attraction pulls you both into the field and the vibration of God's love.

God wants you to know love, feel love, and be the embodiment of love on every level! Yet it is only when we understand that love flows from the heart of God and not from our beloved that we are able to infuse our lives and our beloved with a love that is infinitely *abundant*. This gift of love that God gives us is embedded in how we feel about our beloved in each moment, so we don't have to look outside of ourselves to tap into it. Your desire and affection for your beloved is a powerful way that God's love comes to you and through you. Although the desire is sparked by your beloved's presence, it is important to understand that your beloved is only the key that awakens the flow of love in you. Without this understanding, we are destined to feel empty, to some degree, when our beloved is not present.

Another important understanding is that love can happen only *now*. We experience love as a feeling, and we can feel our feelings only in the present moment. So instead of looking at your relationship as a static thing that doesn't change, think of it as a collection of moments. If the moments are loving, the relationship will be loving. If the moments are a mix of frustrating and loving, then the people in the relationship need to change the kind of moments they are co-creating. The only moment that we can make awesome is this one, so it is important to feel love *right now!* If you act in love, right now, and if you stay in integrity, you will be delighted with the results you create moment-by-moment.

HOW TO BECOME A FREE-FLOWING WELL OF LOVE

The love of God is the most powerful force in the universe. It's what feeds and nurtures our soul, delights us, sparks all our creativity, and heals us. What scares most people about love is that we are also made emotionally vulnerable to our buried hurts in its presence (Bright Lights Cast Dark Shadows). Awesome relationships are essentially the love of God flowing through two hearts that are unhampered by unhealed hurts. Part of making this happen is learning and developing the emotional and relationship skills necessary to be able to consistently enjoy that love and connection.

Love can happen in an instant and it does not require your partner to be present. In fact, it is vital that you be able to feel love whether you are in the presence of your partner or not. Try this practice:

Close your eyes and imagine your partner in front of you. (Imagine an ideal partner if you are not currently in a relation-ship.) Concentrate on an image of your partner that excites you. Feel how you feel when you see him or her in your mind. The key is for you to *feel* the feelings, because this practice doesn't work if you do not feel the feelings. Each time you inhale, imagine your feelings of love filling your lungs. (If you feel like you are just making it up in your imagination, you are doing it right! That's how it works.) With each exhale, imagine blowing your love onto your beloved like a cloud that will wrap your partner up and begin to sink into his or her entire being. With each breath, feel your love a little more, and blow that love onto your beloved.

Now with each inhale, imagine the love of God coming down through the top of your head, flowing into your lungs, and mixing there with the love you have for your beloved. As you exhale, blow this breath of love onto your beloved. Continue to hold in your mind that image of your partner that delights you, and let yourself appreciate all of who he or she is. Blow a breath of appreciation all over this person. In your imagination, say, *Thank you for being here. Thank you for being in my life.* Don't stop with one breath of gratitude. Continue to feel your love and appreciation through many breaths. Continue to blow your love onto your beloved until you can't stand not being with him or her.

Now that you've read the instructions, put this book down. Close your eyes and actually do the practice. No, really—*do the practice now!*

Your body and soul don't know the difference between what you imagine and what is happening in the physical world. When you do this practice, your body chemistry and your emotional chemistry change. You *feel* love! Isn't that what you wanted in the first place, to feel love? Now you can. You just did!

It may not make a difference to the person you were imagining, but it will make a difference in YOU! *You* will feel different! Each moment that you feel love, you are different from the way you were before. Because you are a part of this world, your feeling different makes the world a better place. When you do this practice and you are feeling love, you are the embodiment of love and the embodiment of God's love in this world.

Do this visualization three times a day for the next two weeks, and see the difference it makes in you and in how you respond to your beloved. Then start doing this practice 20 times day, and watch your heart explode with love. You will see people notice your heart like never before. Continuously bring yourself back to this place of feeling love until you recognize it as your natural state. Practice feeling love every day, as much as you can, until it feels normal to feel love and you feel let down when you *stop* feeling love.

Right now, do the practice again, and this time let yourself feel the love even more intensely than you did the first time through. Were you able to feel love again, or did you use up all the love the first time? If you are doing the practice right, you will feel it again the second time through, the third time through, and every time you do it. *God's love is abundant; it doesn't run out.*

When we give love, we become conduits for the love of God to come into this world; that is the teaching of the hollow bone mentioned in Chapter 2. When we feel God's love flowing through us, we are constantly renewed and refilled with love. And according to the Law of Attraction, by feeling love, we are also sending ourselves and the universe a message that love is what we want more of in our lives— we are training ourselves to accept more love and we are training the universe to send more love our way.

The victim mindset is just the opposite. When we are in this mindset, we will always come up with an excuse or a reason not to expand into a larger sense of ourselves. It warns us that giving love is just too much work, and when we give love we run the risk of becoming a doormat who gives love and doesn't get any in return. The victim mindset may whine, *Why do I have to be the one who does all the work?*

This whiny question is worth answering. You have to be the one who does all the work because *you* are the one who wants to be full of love, because *you* are the one who wants to transform your life, and because *you* are the one who came into this world wanting to feel love flowing through you! Here's yet another reason: because doing this work will blow you away. Most people who ask this "why me?" question are coming from a place of being hurt. They were in a relationship where their needs weren't being met and they didn't know how to set appropriate boundaries, or maybe they mistakenly believed that love is limited and they needed to protect themselves at all times. The bottom line is that no one would ask this question if he or she actually knew how much *more* energy returns to the one who sends the love out.

DRIVING PRACTICE

I have a practice that I do every day while I am driving to work. As I negotiate the interstate, I look at all the cars in front of me. I take a deep breath and I imagine that I connect with the heart of each one of the people in the cars I see. "Thank you guys," I say aloud as I drive. "Thank you for driving safely. Thank you for being here in the world. Bless you. I want you to have the best day possible. I love you guys. Go have fun with it today!" Then I blow a big breath of blessing out to the lot of them. Then I look in the rear view mirror, try to take in all the cars behind me, and repeat the same prayer for them.

I don't know if it makes a difference in their lives or if it makes the world a better place, but I do know that it makes a difference in me! I feel better, more compassionate. Bringing that sense of loving kindness to the world makes a difference in how I interact with everyone. If it is love you want, then this practice is for you. When you are in that place of feeling love, you will feel so good to other people that they can't help but love you back!

I try to do some kind of visualization where I feel love at least five or six times an hour. Sometimes it is just a single breath. When I take a break between clients and visualize my wife, when I feel gratitude that she is in my life, when I picture my sister, my brother, my kids, or my parents, I let myself feel the love that I have for them. The aim of this practice is to feel love for anyone, not necessarily just your partner. You can imagine anyone you love and as long as you feel the feelings, the love will transform your life.

When we don't feel love, we often feel an emptiness in our lives. If I am feeling empty, it doesn't bring my wife (or any other good thing) closer to me. Feeling empty just leads to shutting down and feeling despair. But when I feel my love and excitement for my wife, by imagining her presence, it's like I get to drink her in, even when we are apart. Practicing feeling love for her also primes the pump so we can connect more quickly and more deeply when we do see each other.

These visualization exercises can bring on some of the most intense feelings of love you have ever known. Remember the first pillar: It's Not About Joy or Pain, but Intensity. Handling the intensity of the love we feel is not always easy at first. Nearly 75 percent of the people I lead through a loving visualization for the first time make a joke, open their eyes to look around, or deflect in some other way because they are uncomfortable with the intensity. They want the love, but they are not used to feeling their feelings in such a deep, strong way.

Sometimes people feel they are getting out of control when they feel a bigger sense of love. A friend described falling in love as "speeding down the biggest hill in a car with no breaks. You can either jump out of the car and get hurt when you hit the ground, or you can say, 'Thank you, God' and enjoy the ride. But you don't know where love is gonna take you." Essentially, love does indeed render us out of control of some parts of our lives. But problems come only when we try to control the direction love takes us by trying to steer clear of our buried hurts. It is love's job to guide us to those hurt places so they can be healed; it is our job to develop the emotional and relationship skills to be able to heal the hurts and use them to foster more emotional intimacy.

If It Doesn't Feel Good, It Is *Not* Love

Love is love. There is only one kind of love; it is the love of God and it feels *awesome!* When a relationship does not feel good, it is not love that is happening in that moment. If a relationship feels merely okay, that is *not* love either. Love does not feel just okay. Love feels *great!* This doesn't mean the experience of loving won't be scary; it may scare you to death in a really exciting way! You may have to get used to the intensity that love brings. In fact, when the right combination of love and chemistry exists, you *will* have to get used to it! It is more intense than any relationship you have ever had.

When a relationship doesn't feel amazing or wonderful, then something else has taken love's place for the moment, and one of two things is going on: either you are *not* focusing on feeling love or the love that is present has evoked some unhealed pain that is ready to heal (Bright Lights Cast Dark Shadows). Remember, it's not *the love* that is painful, it is the old hurt that is ready to be healed. Rhonda Byrne, author of *The Secret*, describes in her latest book, *The Power,* why we don't feel joyous all the time. Here's how she describes how we use our choice to feel love or to not feel love:

> Most people love and then stop loving hundreds of times in a day. They don't give love long enough for the force of love to move all the good things into their life. Think about it: one moment you give love through a warm hug with a loved one, and then you stop giving love within minutes when you get annoyed because you can't find your keys or you're delayed in traffic or you can't find a parking space. You give love when you laugh with a work colleague, and then stop when you get disappointed because the local lunch place has run out of something you want. You give love as you look forward to the weekend, and then you stop when you receive your bills. And so it continues all through the day; you give love and you stop giving love, give love and stop giving love, give love and stop giving love, from one moment to the next.

The True Nature of Love

Recognize the role your beloved plays in your relationship with God. Your beloved is there, in part, to be a catalyst to help you feel the love of

God. In this way, love is not about your beloved. Your task in this lifetime is to walk the path God has laid out for you. Your beloved is there to help you recognize your sacred path, to encourage you on your path, to support you walking your sacred path, and to keep you connected with the love of God by sparking feelings of love within you. You may, then, think of your beloved as a God-sent gift with the perfectly crafted chemistry you require in order to share in the experience of playing, enjoying, dancing, healing, and loving in the waterfall of God's love. Conversely, your partner may be just the opposite—someone who calls you to take a hard look at yourself and what you have asked for in your life. If so, you may be settling for less than you deserve, and it's time to heal the hurts that are getting in the way of you getting what you really desire in life.

No matter what kind of relationship we are in, the love we feel is the same. Sure, we feel differently about a friendship than we do a romantic relationship, but those differences are based in our thoughts, feelings, beliefs, and expectations about the relationship, not the love itself. If we strip away our attitudes and thoughts about a close friendship, we will experience a love just as whole and fulfilling as the most intimate romance. The love in a close, intimate friendship will impact us differently than the love of an intimate romance because it is a different type of relationship, but the love is just as big, just as thrilling, just as healing, and just as touching.

The difference will be in the chemistry of the relationship. In order to make sure that we step into love in all types of relationships, God gives us the gift of chemistry with others—the excitement that makes us want to get closer and create more intimacy. Romantic feelings are created by romantic chemistry. Sexual desire is created by sexual chemistry. Friendship chemistry is what drives us to get closer to our friends. We don't normally think of liking a friend as a type of chemistry, even though we react to it by creating friendships just as we react to romantic chemistry by creating romantic relationships. The feelings in a friendship are uniquely "friendly," but the process of loving the ones we love is the same.

Because these different types of chemistry create different types of relationships, recognizing and differentiating between the different types of feelings we have when we are strongly attracted to people is vitally important. When we can recognize the type of chemistry for what it is and be clear about what it is *not*, then we can allow ourselves to feel the deeper richness of all our relationships.

Differentiating between sexual chemistry and romantic chemistry can be really hard for a lot of people (and impossible for others). It *is* possible to have one without the other, although many of us are brought up to believe that these two different energies are the same or *should* only go together. But they are not the same and don't always coincide. Many couples have one or the other and wonder why they do not feel fulfilled in their relationship.

To demonstrate the importance of differentiating between the different types of chemistry, I want to share the story of several couples whose marriages ended in an identical way. Several of my female clients have gotten divorced after their husbands had affairs (and then married the "other" women with whom they were not really "in love"). In each of these particular cases, the men could not differentiate between romantic chemistry, sexual chemistry, and the close friendship they felt with the other woman. The men felt an incredibly close friendship with these other women and felt a great deal of sexual chemistry, as well, but they did not feel any romantic chemistry and found out later that they also shared no lifestyle chemistry.

In each case, the men had an affair that was driven by the sexual chemistry, then came home, confessed to the affair, began divorce proceedings, and married the other woman as quickly as possible. Oddly, *none* of their original wives sensed any significant problems before the affair, and all of the men later agreed that no problems existed in the marriage beyond normal marital issues. The men simply shut down and began pushing their wives away. In every one of these cases, when I suggested to the original wives, my clients, that their husbands had friendship chemistry and sexual chemistry with these other women, they each looked dumbfounded and told me that explanation totally fit.

"That poor stupid bastard," one of the women said. "He had a fling and instead of coming home and telling me that he screwed up. He had to justify it and act like she was the one he was meant to be with. What an idiot! Don't get me wrong, I would have killed him, but at least we would've been real about it."

In each case, the women realized that their husbands freaked out when they came home because they couldn't make sense of what they were feeling. Each of the husbands had strong convictions about remaining faithful in marriage and when they had affairs, they couldn't make sense of it. The men felt like they needed to "make it right" somehow, or at least justify their infidelity. The peculiar outcome in each of these cases was that the husbands were fairly miserable in the new marriages because the romantic chemistry and lifestyle chemistry weren't there.

Sexual chemistry is a way to feel love. Everyone wants to feel love; the task is to be clear about how you want to feel love. Do you want only the sexual? Do you want only the friendship plus the sexual (commonly known as "friends with benefits")? Do you want a friend with whom you can live comfortably and have a great friendship? Or do you want it all—a relationship with all four types of chemistry?

God has given us the gift of different types of chemistry to enjoy different types of relationships. Each of these different types of relationships holds a special type of blessing in our lives. The common thread in each different kind of relationship is the love we feel with and for each other. That love is a gift. Our task is to stay open and be excited by the chemistry, feel the love, and maintain the relationship skills to keep each different relationship in our life as healthy as possible.

WHEN YOU ARE FIGHTING

If you and your beloved are at odds, you have a choice to feel love or not. You can choose to view and treat your partner in a way that fuels the feeling of love or in a way that fuels the emotional distance, fear, disconnect, and/or hurt. Which one would you rather choose?

Why should you choose to hold a loving image of your partner in your mind even when you are angry with this person for something he or she has done? Because the alternative stinks! The alternative is to *not* feel your love for your partner. *Not* feeling your love doesn't bring the two of you any closer together, doesn't heal any hurts, and doesn't help either of you to resolve any issues between you. I am not suggesting you ignore your hurt feelings or pretend you're not angry—not at all. I am saying that when you are angry or hurt, your love is still a valid part of what is going on and it needs to be felt and communicated.

One of the biggest problems that couples face is how they treat each other when they are angry. It is possible to be angry and still treat your partner lovingly. So many people believe being angry is a justification for treating their partner hatefully, when they don't actually hate their partners. Most people have not been taught that when they're upset, they can be loving and accepting *and also* be firm in expressing what is important to them. This is the key to resolving conflicts!

When we get angry, it is because we perceive that we have been wronged in some way or because we are scared—sometimes both. If we justify treating our partner hatefully because we are too scared to look at what fear is lurking underneath our anger, we stay stuck in our pain. But when we instead choose to get in touch with the hidden hurt or fear, then we have the opportunity to address the issue in a better way, deepening our emotional intimacy with our partner and enhancing our personal growth.

AFFECTION AND SEX IS A CELEBRATION (NOT THE CURRENCY) OF LOVE

In one way, romantic affection should come only when we don't *need* it. It would then be a pure celebration of how we feel together with our beloved. When we know our own lovable-ness, we can more fully celebrate the love we have. Of course, affection is wonderful any time, we all love it, and you can never have too much of it when it's genuine. Here's the point: When we don't *need* it (because all our emotional needs have been met), then we are free to *enjoy* it ("joy" being the operative part of "enjoy"). When two people make love in any way, whether through sex, hugging, kissing, cuddling, or playing, and they are both full of love and feel no sense of lack in their hearts, then the love they make is transformative.

A Native American medicine woman once told me that we are never closer to God than when we are making love. This explains why sex is so exciting and so much a part of our culture. We are all longing to become enlightened and know God on some level! The sad part is that the lack of understanding we have about our sexuality, the lack of integrity we have around sex, and lack of healthy boundaries we draw around sex has led to sex becoming such a taboo—which only adds to the shame so many people feel around their sexuality.

In Chapter 2, we discussed how the emotional opening that love brings leads to our unhealed hurts coming to the forefront. Healing those hurts paves the way for authentic closeness, which allows us to feel the blessing of God's presence in our lives. We experience the love of God through our own feelings, *including* our sexual feelings. When the hurts have healed, love and sex both feel like really great parties where the spiritual and physical energies dance together wonderfully!

When people talk to me about their relationships, they sometimes describe "running out of love," and imply that they can be full of love only when they receive affection from their beloved. When they're low on love, it's as if they think they need to go back to the well and fill up on affection again. This sets up the dynamic of taking something from their partner, being dependent on the affection they receive, and possibly making sex and affection an indicator of how loved they feel. When sex or affection becomes a symbol that we are loved, then we miss out on the spiritual gifts they have to offer us.

Relationships do not exist to meet our needs for validation or confirmation, although relationships *do* bring those needs to the surface so they can be healed. I know that sounds like a paradox, and it is an important distinction to make. The danger comes when we look only to our partner to heal our buried hurts for us. This creates an imbalance in the relationship, because each of us needs to have the resources to heal our hurts instead of expecting our loved ones to magically do it for us. Those resources are both internal (the emotional skills necessary for healthy relationships) and external (social support and a good therapist or relationship coach).

We all give and take a little bit in relationships, and that's okay. When we are appreciated and appreciative, the give and take is usually not a problem. But when we are coming from a place of lack, then we are, in essence, asking our partner to give us something that we take away with us. This is not a model for long-term balance or long-term growth in the relationship.

When someone gives you something with strings attached, it feels horrible. One model of relationship counseling holds that for every piece you take away from your partner either in love or in harshness, you must give a piece back in love. For example, if you say something mean to your partner, you must make up for it by saying something nice. The downside of this approach is that when you do something nice for your partner, it becomes acceptable to then do something mean or aggravating, or to feel like he or she owes you something. This is stupid. It may keep one person from using the other, but both people stay emotionally bankrupt. It's far better to draw and enforce healthy boundaries that will keep people like that out of your life than assure they "pay you back."

When I first heard this coin-for-a-coin philosophy, I asked, "Why give just one? Why not give four for every one that I take? Why not give five, or six, or a hundred?" In fact, why take anything? Why not just enjoy my beloved, appreciate her, adore her, support her, listen to her, worship her as the goddess she is in my life, and give thanks *to* her and *for* her? When she does give to me, I appreciate it greatly! So why not consider everything I give to her as a giveaway?

If I give and want to take in equal amounts, that is not being a husband, that is being a *creditor!* "I gave to you. Now, give it back!" If I am an affection creditor, then it creates the possibility that I have to pursue and possibly harass my partner when she has not paid her affection debts to me—or maybe I will consider any lack of affection as proof that I am not worthy or lovable. That is not love. That is trying to get *other* needs met in the relationship. (We will discuss more about what some of those *other* needs are later in this chapter and again in detail in Chapter 5 and Chapter 6.)

What's needed is a balanced approach, but by "balanced" I don't mean giving and taking equally—I mean being balanced within yourself, so that you are not dependent on your partner to maintain your desired level of vitality, spirituality, emotionality, or physicality. Being balanced means feeling your own feelings of love, which taps you into an exciting source of energy, from which in turn you can give *freely*. In his moving and heartfelt song "Break in the Cup," David Wilcox sings: "We can't trade empty for empty.... We must go to the waterfall." What he means is that our human frailties keep us from being able to generate the love necessary to fill each other up. It is only in holding our cup under the waterfall of God's love that we may always have the love we need.

BREAK UPS

So often we have a difficult time with the ending of a relationship. A big part of the struggle is the fear that when the relationship ends, the love ends, too. We are afraid that losing a partner will mean losing the love and possibly our lovable-ness, as if our partner's love is what makes us lovable. We will undoubtedly confront other hurts in the break-up, but this does not need to be one of them.

When we recognize that love flows from the heart of God, then we understand that losing our beloved does not threaten our ability to receive love. When we stay in the flow of God's love, heartbreak is much more manageable. So often, I see people who stay in bad relationships because they do not want to lose one of two things: feeling safety and security (which we will discuss in Chapter 5) or feeling self-worth, acceptance, and/or confirmation (which we will discuss in Chapter 6).

The death of a loved one or the death of a relationship can rock us to the core; there is no denying that. Some seem to get stuck in the grief, seemingly taking forever to heal from the loss. This is because they have not let themselves feel the intensity of their pain. Often they are scared the pain is too great and they cannot survive it. Chapter 1 covered how love can force people to open up to an intensity of feeling they may not be used to and how shutting down protects them from feeling pain. Death can have the same effect, but in the reverse order. When a loved one dies, people can either shut down (a terrible option with terrible consequences, but an option nonetheless) or face feeling an intense pain that evokes all other pain that they have buried and not healed.

One client who is a self-professed code monkey (computer programmer) summed it up like this: "So when someone dies, it initiates a cache dump, and everything that I have stuffed down and never dealt with gets dumped all at once. Except it doesn't get thrown out, it gets thrown up! We just start vomiting our pain for everything that has ever happened to us, right? We just spew it all over everyone."

"Exactly! Well said," I responded. "The only thing I would add is this: While we start feeling every bit of buried hurt we haven't yet healed, we only get the *pain* of the old hurt, not the *content* of the old hurt. So when someone dies, all the hurt that comes up *feels* like it is all about the recent loss."

The visualization practice described earlier in this chapter can transform grief. Because our souls are made up of pure love, it is only when we feel love that we get to experience one another on a soul-to-soul level. When we die, only our bodies die, not our souls. Our souls still exist; they simply don't reside in a body anymore. When we feel love for those who have died, we raise our vibration to the same frequency where they exist now. It is only when we feel our love for those we have lost that we get to experience the connection we still have with them. When we feel our love for them, they are not lost to us anymore.

In order to feel nothing but love for those who have died, we have to accept the death of their bodies. We have to be okay with never seeing them again in the same way as we did when their bodies were alive. When my father died, I was ready for him to die because his body was in horrible shape. I didn't *want* him to die. I wanted him back healthy, the way I remembered him, and I knew that was not going to happen. He had lived almost ten years longer than expected and had steadily declined with almost no chance of recovery. It sucked! It still sucks because I have so much I want to share with him.

But here's what I do about it. I have an image of him in my mind that reminds me of the part of him that I love. I hold that image of him in my imagination and feel how much I love him. I tell him that I love him. I imagine him seeing everything in my life that I want to share, and I invite him to give me feedback (although I have not received any yet). The remarkable thing is that when I feel my love for him, I feel his presence and *I do not feel any loss.* My skeptical mind says, *Oh Marcus, you must be avoiding the pain. You are kidding yourself.* Yet I do feel pain from time to time, and as much as I hate feeling the pain, I welcome it. I trust that feeling the pain only brings me more fully into the world because feeling and healing pain leaves that much more of me open to love and be of service to the people who need me. I want that for you, too.

So practice feeling love every day! Use the imagery practice in this chapter as a starting point for increasing your capacity to feel love. When you notice a block that prevents you from feeling love, *feel it!* Get to know it! Find out what story it has to tell. Test the upper limits of love—ask for the love you want and for the love you need, and let that much love flow through you for anything and everything in the world. As you begin to feel a love that is more than you ever thought possible, also let yourself feel loved more than you ever thought possible.

THE FOUR PILLARS AT WORK

Now that we've discussed each of the Four Pillars of Awesome Relationships (It's Not About Joy or Pain, but Intensity; Bright Lights Cast Dark Shadows; Hurt Feelings Are Like Rowdy Teenagers; and Love is Not About Your Beloved—Love is Feeling The Heart of God), I want to share a story that illustrates how each of the four pillars played a part in a woman's healing. Recently, I led this woman through a guided meditation intended to help her get a clear sense of what it feels like to feel love separate from receiving affection. This woman lives with an almost constant feeling that she is going to lose her boyfriend and lose the love she gets from him. I wanted to pick something really easy for her to love—her new kitten—for this first time doing the meditation. As I guided her through a practice similar to the one described earlier in this chapter, she easily began to feel illuminated.

"I have so much love to share," she said when we were done. "I can't wait to share it with my boyfriend when I get home. Halfway through the meditation, I switched from my cat to my boyfriend and I started feeling how connected we really are. Marcus," she added as a look of wonder washed over her, "I don't have to be afraid! I can do this!"

"Is your boyfriend an idiot?" I asked.

"No" she said, laughing.

"He would have to be an idiot to walk away from the kind of love you just tapped into. How do you feel right now?"

"I feel like I am glowing. *I can do this.*"

"You *are* glowing," I told her. "And yes, you *can* do this." She was radiating love, and for the first time in her life, she felt like a happy, close, loving relationship was possible for her. We talked for a few minutes, integrating the work she had just done, and then all of a sudden, her face went dark. She looked pained and tears began to roll down her cheeks. She slowly crossed her arms across her stomach and bent over on the couch.

"I have never felt wanted," she bemoaned. "I have never felt loved" (Bright Lights Cast Dark Shadows). When she opened up to a higher vibration of love than she had ever experienced before, it brought up a hurt that had been trying to come out to heal.

For the rest of the day and into the night, she had to weather a pretty harsh emotional storm. Then she called and left a message telling me she had gained the insight that she had spent her whole life creating dramas that left her feeling abandoned. Without realizing it, she had lived her life trying to make her hurt feelings go away by distracting herself (Hurt Feelings Are Like Rowdy Teenagers).

She also said in the message that she now realized she was safe with her boyfriend and she was not going to run away from feeling the pain anymore. While she was feeling the love initially, during the visualization, she let herself feel it as intensely as the love came. And then later that night, when the pain came, she let herself feel it as intensely as the pain came, asking her boyfriend to hold her. When the pain matured into her being able to be more present than she ever had been, the storm of emotions passed (It's Not About Joy or Pain, but Intensity).

The following morning, she sent me an e-mail saying that she felt a shift. She'd been sitting at her desk for 90 minutes that morning and had hardly wavered from feeling love for her boyfriend or her cat the entire time. When she did feel her love drop, she re-focused on each of them and felt the sense of love come back quickly. She was allowing herself to be a conduit and feel love, not just receive affection like a drug that would wear off (Love Is Not about Your Beloved—Love Is Feeling the Heart of God).

I am glad to report that this client is now happily married. Her fear of abandonment still gets triggered from time to time, and she has learned to handle the fear in a really good way. She no longer uses food and affection as a drug to medicate the fear; instead, she shares the hurt feelings with her husband in a way that doesn't push him away and that gives both of them the chance to be closer.

PRACTICES:

- For the next two weeks, do the loving visualization practice outlined earlier in this Chapter 3 times a day for two minutes each time. After two weeks, you should be pretty adept at feeling your love and you will be able to "drop in" more quickly, so from then on, aim to do the practice 20 times a day for 30 seconds each time—for the rest of your life! Here's a recap: Hold an image in your mind of your partner that excites you. Imagine with each breath that your lungs are filling up with the love that you feel for your partner, and then blow this breath of love onto him or her. Then imagine the love of God coming down through the top of your head and mixing in your lungs with your love, and blow this breath onto you partner. Remember, this practice doesn't work if you are not feeling the feelings; and if you feel as if you are just making it up in your head, you are doing it right!

- Choose a loved one who has passed away and do the same loving visualization, holding in your mind an image of the person from one of your favorite memories. Feel your love for the other person, and allow yourself to feel more and more love as you breathe. With each exhale, blow a breath of love onto your loved one and thank him or her for touching your life.

- Regularly do the driving practice described earlier in this chapter, *but only when you can do it while driving safely!* To recap, imagine connecting with the heart of someone in a random car in front of you. Let yourself feel gratitude that he or she is here on the planet at this time. Welcome that person to the world the way you would a newborn baby. Imagine you are speaking directly into his or her heart and say, "Thank you for being here. Thank you for driving safely. I want you to have a blessed day and feel the love of God dancing inside you." Then blow a blessing breath of love and imagine that breath going directly onto the other person in his or her car. Repeat this practice every time you get into a car.

PART TWO:

THE 12 MOST COMMON PITFALLS OF RELATIONSHIPS

Chapter 5

Is the World Okay?

In Part One, the discussion of the Four Pillars of Awesome Relationships, I constantly referred to pain, hurt, or some other uncomfortable emotion that can be evoked by getting closer to your beloved. Now, in this chapter and the next, I'll talk about what the majority of those hurts are, where they come from, and why these issues are so pervasive in our lives.

How It Is Supposed to Be

I want to start by taking a look at what our lives would have been like if our parents had done a *perfect* job as parents. How would things be different for us if we had been set up for nothing but the most incredible love and the most amazing life? If we set our goal to feel love as if we were born of love itself, without putting an upper limit on love or happiness, then we stay open for awesome things to happen. In a perfect world, we would be flooded with love from the moment we are conceived. We would feel at all times as though we were made of love itself. Love is our natural state; it is our birthright.

Perry Robinson, minister, wise man, and co-founder of the Center for Peace in Seymour, Tennessee, once told me: "We come from a place of pure love before we are born and return to a place of pure love when our bodies die. Our job in this lifetime is to remember how to love each other and ourselves the way God loves us while we are here. If we are lucky, we never forget how to do that after we are born." Perry went on to tell the story of a mother who overheard her four-year-old talking to her infant brother in his crib. "I need you to learn to talk soon so you can tell me what it's like," the older child said, "because I am starting to forget." The four-year-old recognized that she was forgetting what it was like to be in that place of pure love—the place we live before coming to this world.

We are supposed to be showered in love so we never have a doubt about the divine grace of the world or the divine grace that we truly are. As we grow, we are supposed to gain age-appropriate responsibility while carrying the abundant love from our parents and family with us in everything we do. We are supposed to be honored so thoroughly and completely that as we encounter difficult situations, the thoughts, *I am all alone, I don't belong,* or even *I suck* never even enter our awareness. Imagine if when we're faced with a problem, every possible solution that comes to our minds were infused with love and respect while naturally enforcing healthy boundaries.

What came up for you reading the last paragraph? What I usually hear is a sarcastic, "Yeah, in a perfect world!" Well, most of us didn't get a perfect childhood. In fact, most of us got something *very* far from it. You may feel like you barely survived your early years. But in truth, you did more that survive—you survived with your heart intact. You made it! And you are good enough! Your heart is still longing for more passion and connection in your life. Not only do you deserve that passion and connection, but it's also possible for you to get it!

Now that we are adults, we can't ask our parents or our families to set right the wrongs that were done. We might occasionally get an apology from a parent for something he or she did or said, but those apologies can be few and far between, if they come at all. Instead, we have to find what we need elsewhere, and that process begins with taking responsibility for our wounds. Even though we didn't create the wounds from our childhood, we have to take the responsibility to heal them now as adults.

WHY TALK ABOUT EARLY CHILDHOOD DEVELOPMENT?

Unhealed hurts from childhood and the emotional habits we developed in response to those hurts are, in one way or another, the cause of every divorce, break up, and argument any of us have ever had. So it's important that we heal them, both for our own happiness and also because we each have a responsibility to leave this world a better place than we found it. We need to create a better emotional environment in which the next generations can grow.

The startling truth is that the foundation for a healthy emotional life is laid by the age of three. That means that if our emotional needs are not met by then, they can remain unmet for the rest of our lives, leaving us emotionally hungry and needy—*unless we heal!* Having the solid foundation that comes from having our early childhood needs met is like having a healthy immune system for everyday hurts; when we heal our early childhood wounding, we are much less susceptible to the harsh words of others and we can respond appropriately, with compassion, embodying the very best version of ourselves. We are also much less susceptible to doubt, nearly immune to the fear of losing love, intolerant of emotional drama, and more capable of handling major life stresses like serious conflict, divorce, and death.

In almost every conflict that couples bring to me, they are feeling a type of frustration that comes from having a grown-up body, grown-up lifestyle, grown-up sense of rationality, grown-up communication patterns, grown-up job, and grown-up finances along with the emotional skills of a three-year-old! Three-year-olds don't know how to express their hurts, so they play games, lie, ignore, throw temper tantrums, pout, and do spiteful things to get the attention they need. Adults who didn't learn as children how to appropriately express themselves when they're unhappy still use these childish ways of trying to get their needs met. That's why the problems that most people face—from politics to romance—probably stem from experiences they had in their first three years of life.

ATTACHMENT

Attachment matters for two big reasons. First, the quality of our early attachment to a caregiver gives us a lens through which we view ourselves, the world, and all of our relationships. The view through this lens affects how we feel and how we respond to pretty much everything. Second, attachment wounds, no matter how small, make us tend to avoid emotional vulnerability—which is absolutely necessary for deeper intimacy.

Understanding and healing our own attachment issues gives us a solid emotional foundation that opens the door for us to be loving, responsible, and proactive rather than guarded with our lovers, children, families, friends, and ultimately our communities. This means that as we heal, we will begin to have a healthy perspective on the safety and security of being in the world as well as a great sense of love, trust, and belonging.

Right now, ask yourself the question, "Is the world okay?" Be honest with yourself. Next, rate the world on a scale of 1 to 10 in terms of its awesomeness, where 1 is bad and 10 is incredibly awesome. Now give yourself a rating from 1 to 10 on each of the following questions:

- How safe do I feel in the world?
- How secure do I feel in the world?
- How easy is it for me to give love?
- How easy is it for me to receive love?
- How easily do I trust others?
- How easily do others trust me?

Your answers to all of these questions were determined by how your primary caregivers (usually your parents) cared for you and responded to you, as well as by how much healing work you have already done as an adult. This creates a subconscious emotional template that you use to perceive and respond to the world and to determine how deeply you are willing to engage with others.

Recently, a client brought her ten-month-old child along with her for a session. As the mother and I talked, the baby played on the floor, ignoring her mother and occasionally munching on dry Cheerios. Every five or six minutes, the cute little rug rat would make a sound and look to see if her mom was looking at her. If the mother made eye contact, the baby returned to playing and the whole process would begin again. In this case, the child did not need physical touch, she just needed eye contact. If the mother did not immediately make eye contact, the baby would make another sound, this time a little bit louder. If that did not get eye contact from the mother, the child would begin moving toward the mother and making whining noises. In my house, we call those "mommy checks." The mother's attentiveness makes the child feel secure and safe and gives the child a sense of belonging. If this mother had not been so attentive, the little one would have begun to cry, when all she really needed in the first place was eye contact from her mom.

As you can see, there is an incredible demand on primary caregivers to be attentive. If a parent is constantly in distress or otherwise *not* emotionally attentive, then the child may not be soothed by the parent's presence and doesn't learn to regulate his or her own emotions. The degree to which the parents respond in a warm and soothing way when an infant is in any kind of distress determines the degree to which the child grows up feeling free not only to express love, receive love, and develop a healthy sense of trust, but also to express frustration, anger, and fear in a healthy, non-destructive way—without being afraid of being judged or rejected.

If a child consistently has to cry or even rage in order to get food or attention, he or she can develop a type of hair trigger with any sort of physical or emotional discomfort. With the slightest bit of hunger, the child learns to throw a fit immediately because he or she has learned that mild attempts to get a caregiver's attention will not work—screaming is what gets results.

This is entirely normal for an infant, and in fact, an infant's survival could depend on it. An infant shouldn't be concerned about how her caretaker feels if the caretaker is neglecting the child. However, an adult who responds without concern for other people's feelings is a huge problem! This same emotional habit continued into adulthood is destructive because those who display it are more concerned with alleviating their own discomfort than considering anyone else's feelings. This translates into teens and adults who immediately blow a gasket or create a drama in which every time they feel uncomfortable, they see themselves as victims.

Attachment issues also show up in adults through a long list of other behaviors, such as:

- needing constant attention and affirmation, and being clingy with a romantic partner
- accusing loved ones of not loving them and whining when no one is close—and then pushing those same loved ones away when they do come close
- taking care of everyone but themselves
- shutting down their feelings until they eventually explode
- acting aggressively and then isolating themselves
- avoiding taking responsibility for their actions or being defensive and thus avoiding being emotionally vulnerable
- experiencing anxiety and/or depression
- having drug, alcohol, sex, and/or other addictions
- feeling as if they don't belong or their voice doesn't matter
- having issues with authority
- needing to control everything
- having difficulty asking for help and/or being excessively self-reliant

- getting frustrated easily and displaying intense anger and hostility
- not being able to communicate well or resolve conflicts
- being physically and/or emotionally abusive
- blaming everyone else
- having difficulty accepting love and/or establishing trust
- seeing themselves as either unlovable or too good for others

As we mature, attachment patterns become unconscious, pervasive attitudes that govern how we approach and respond to the world. In essence, these attitudes answer the question, "Is the world okay?" Our experience with attachment is also reflected in our answers to a few other questions, as well, including:

- Is it okay for me to show up in the world and let people see who I really am?
- Can I trust someone will be there for me when I ask for help?
- Is expressing my frustrations a waste of time? Will it change anything?
- Am I all alone in the world?
- Is the whole world out to get me?

ATTACHMENT IN ADULT RELATIONSHIPS

The three main needs infants have that affect their emotional makeup as adults are *food*, *touch*, and *movement*. Meeting the attachment needs of infants is simple; give them the food, touch, and movement they need, when they need it, and do it lovingly. Working with teens and adults is different, since as adults we can pretty much take care of those needs for ourselves. What actually happens as people grow up, though, is that those basic needs of food, touch, and movement get translated into slightly different needs—*nurturing, contact,* and *emotional responsibility* (respectively). Let's take a look at each of them.

Nurturing: Generally, we think of nurturing as only relating to children. The truth is that we all need nurturing, often through support from one another and especially from our partners. If we as adults are open to the nurturing we need and are willing to accept it, we are more attuned to recognizing and providing a safe, comfortable environment for others when the need arises.

When I asked my wife about nurturing recently, she commented: "If I ignore my need to make the whole world about me in a good way every now and then, like taking a long, hot bath after getting a massage every month, then I start to make everything about me in a really ugly way by creating dramas about everything."When we ignore our need for nurturing, our souls cry out for care, just like a rowdy teenager.

Contact: This is heart-to-heart connection, soul-to-soul connection with awareness. In order to make deeper emotional contact, we usually have to break a lot of habits that we have adopted that otherwise keep us at a certain emotional distance where we can avoid showing up more fully. Making such deep emotional contact isn't always comfortable because it can force us to be vulnerable, which requires us to feel safe and have a sense of security even when we don't feel in control.

It is in our early development that we learn to make or break deep emotional contact by the modeling that our parents provide. When we become more comfortable with making genuine, heart-to-heart contact with our lovers, our interactions become more authentic and more loving—and as we saw in Chapter 2, authenticity is one of the foundational pieces of spiritual enlightenment.

Emotional Responsibility: People who take responsibility for their own emotions are the coolest people on the planet, which is why I named this the *Fonzi Method*. Arthur Fonzarelli (also known as "Fonzi") from the '70s television show *Happy Days* had the cool catchphrase, "AAAAEEEEEEEEEEEEEEEEEE." Nobody knew what it meant when Fonzi said this, but everyone knew that he was the coolest guy on the planet when he did. When Fonzi's catchphrase is shortened to "AAE," it gives us an acronym for how to achieve emotional responsibility:

A – Awareness

A – Acceptance

E – Expression

Emotional Awareness: Emotional awareness is knowing what we're feeling as we are feeling it. As simple as this sounds, some of us have a hard time with it. Most often, when I ask someone how he or she feels, the person will respond with an *evaluation* of the feeling, not the feeling itself. "Good," "fine," and "okay" are not feelings. Feelings basically fall into four rough categories: mad, sad, glad, or afraid. When you share with your beloved how you actually feel, your relationship gets deeper— and conversely, if you don't, it won't.

The deepest, most profound implications of emotional awareness include knowing that our feelings are created entirely by our own internal processes. So when we're emotionally aware, we recognize that no external forces, circumstances, people, or places have caused us to feel bad. We know what we are feeling *and* that we have created our feelings in response to our environment. We own the fact that our feelings are nothing more than *our responses* to what is going on around us, and we acknowledge that we have a choice in how we respond.

Emotional Acceptance: Emotional acceptance is knowing that it's okay to feel what we are feeling. No matter what we are feeling, even if we don't like it, it is vital to accept that we are feeling it. None of us wants to feel hurt, shame, anger, jealousy, fear, and so on. But accepting the fact that we are feeling it and accepting ourselves for feeling it are both crucial for our emotional health. Without that, we can't communicate authentically.

Not accepting how we are feeling does not change how we are feeling, it simply keeps us from being real. Even when we are confronting things we don't like to feel—such as shame and guilt—being aware that we're having those feelings is vital. *Emotional acceptance is not about judging how we are feeling, it's about judging whether or not we are feeling it.*

Emotional Expression: Emotional expression is sharing how we feel with another person, in a good way, as we are feeling it. Great relationships are based on effective emotional communication—in fact, without it, we can't have true intimacy. The simplest example of communicating an emotion is to say, "I feel _____." I often challenge couples to only make "feeling" statements for a week. It is amazing how much we can express while only stating our feelings and desires.

Emotional expression is *not* about what we think. "I feel you are insensitive," is not a feeling statement. That's stating an opinion. However, "I feel annoyed when I feel like you don't hear me," *is* a feeling statement. To be able to express what we feel, we of course must first be aware of what it is we are feeling—that's why this is the last step in the Fonzi Method.

A couple in their mid-30s sat in my office talking about an argument they'd had about money the day before. Shortly after they began talking about the fight, they started fighting again in my office. The husband kept saying, "You shouldn't spend so much money. You spend too much money." These statements felt like attacking criticism to his wife, and she felt like he was trying to control her. Both of these feelings struck a nerve, an unhealed hurt, from her childhood.

She did what most people do when they feel attacked: she defended herself. To that end, she began justifying her spending habits, but to her husband, this just discounted all of his arguments about why she shouldn't spend so much money. In turn, this outraged him because he felt like she didn't care about their finances, which was something he often worried about. Not surprisingly, the argument got pretty heated, pretty fast.

When I intervened, I asked him how he was feeling at the exact moment when he realized she had spent money the day before. "She spends too much money," he replied. I said that he had not expressed a feeling. He did a half eye roll and said, "*I feel* like she spends too much money." I sarcastically commended him for using the feeling statement form and again pointed out that he had not expressed a feeling. I offered: mad, sad, glad, or afraid. I asked him to take a moment to take a few breaths and check-in with his gut. After he did this, he admitted, "I was scared."

What followed was beautiful. Once he quit trying to win the argument with his wife, he was able to get in touch with the real issue underneath their financial argument. He went on to say that when she spends money, he feels pressure to make more. His business is struggling due to a shift in his industry's technology and he is scared that his business might fail. I asked him to make eye contact with his wife and tell her how scared he is.

He looked at her and made a sort of apologetic smile and said, "I want you to be able to spend all the money you want. I don't want you to even have to think about it. And right now, I am so scared that we are going to lose everything. I feel so much pressure to provide for us. I want to provide so much and I am scared our whole business is going to fail. When you spend money, I get mad because it feels like another reminder of how close to losing everything we are." Then he continued, his voice softening even more, "It feels like just another one of my daily reminders that I am a failure."

By sharing his feelings at a deeper level, the tone of the conversation shifted from argumentative to compassionate. She immediately warmed up to him and moved to sit closer to him, and then she apologized for spending so much. She acknowledged that she had spent a lot of money that was not necessary and that she didn't know he felt so much stress. The two had dropped into a place of close emotional connection, the intimacy was palpable, and I found myself smiling for them.

In his book, *Self-concept: The Enemy Within*, Kevin Everett FitzMaurice describes the ways in which people change how they speak in relationships once they begin to accept responsibility for their feelings:

> They learn to drop expressions from their speech that show dis-ownership of feelings and a helpless or victim attitude towards their feelings. Expressions such as: "They made me feel . . ." "It

made me feel . . ." "I made them feel . . ." and any others that denote external emotional responsibility are first changed into "I" statements as opposed to "you" or blaming statements. They are, for example, changed from, "You make me so mad when you do that," to "I feel mad when you do that because . . . ." People learn at this level to regularly use the following expressions: "When you did . . . , I felt . . . , because . . . ." "When . . . happened, I felt . . . , because . . . ."

Many of the examples you will read in this book show how authentic communication fosters intimacy. Verbally expressing our loving emotions with each other is vital, and the crucial first step is really understanding and practicing emotionally responsible communication. We must begin with emotional awareness and emotional acceptance. If those first two skills of the Fonzi Method are not in place, we will keep failing at the third (emotional expression) and our communication will be devoid of the vulnerability that's necessary for true intimate emotional expression.

THE BIG QUESTION

The lesson of this chapter can be boiled down to one question: Are you willing to let the world love you, to love it back, to fully show up, and to make the enlightening power of love a part of your awareness? If parents create an environment of emotional distance and/or abuse and neglect, their children may never know that the world can be any other way, and the coping strategies they adopt will have nothing to do with love. Children do not have the mental capacity and perspective to understand that the view of the world that an anxious, dismissive, self-absorbed, or angry parent creates is not necessarily the whole picture. But because that is the only world that these children know, they will grow up creating lives and relationships that carry the same insecure, unsafe, and untrusting feelings.

Most people keep trying to find that "special fit" in a partner that makes up for what they did not get from their parents *or* they find someone who relates to them in a similar way as their parents, in an effort to heal those parental wounds. As they heal and begin to meet their core needs, they start to get a sense of feeling settled and secure, giving them a foundation for being able to live the kind of life they truly want to live. When they heal their attachment issues, they become willing for the first time to let others be emotionally close, letting go of being clingy, angry, or distant. The biggest and probably most profound difference is when people begin to risk being more loving with their partners in situations where they would have never felt safe allowing themselves to feel these more tender feelings before.

PRACTICES:

- For the next seven days, only make feeling statements. Challenge yourself to make this work. When in doubt, feel how you feel about someone or what you want to feel with the other person and share that. To ask a question (to find out where someone would like to eat or how the other person is feeling, for example) using feeling statements, try something like this: "I am curious to know what you would like for dinner," or "I would love to know how you are feeling right now."

- Let yourself be held. Find someone who feels "bigger" than you in some way and ask him or her for a hug. Take a breath while you are being hugged and feel what it feels like to be held. Then let yourself feel it a little more.

- Make and maintain eye contact with someone whom you care about and make an effort to look deeper into that person and invite him or her to look deeper into you. Pay attention to what feelings come up as you do this practice. Share those feelings, stating them as feelings. (For example: "As I looked deeper into you, I got worried that you might be frightened of being so vulnerable," or "As I felt you looking deeper into me, I got scared that you wouldn't really like me if you knew the *real* me.")

- Identify two or three feelings that you have that you don't like having. Share those feelings with someone close to you. (For example: "I feel _____. I don't like that I feel this way sometimes, and I don't want to hide from the truth anymore.")

CHAPTER 6

AM I OKAY?

While waiting to pick up my son from elementary school one day, I sat in my car with the windows down. Some fourth graders, the oldest kids in this school at about age nine, walked past me on their way to their bus. Two boys were walking together, with a third boy walking slightly behind the other two. "OOOOOhhhhh, Gaaawwwd," the tallest, one of those in front, exclaimed loudly to the one trailing behind. "You are soooo immature!" His tone obviously intended this as an insult conveying, "I am better than you/more mature than you."

Ironically, teasing someone about being immature is actually an act of immaturity itself. Here's why: The cognitive capacity to understand a concept like maturity doesn't develop until the ages of eight or nine. The roots of self-esteem are planted by the age of three. In order to emotionally mature past the age of three, a child must develop a healthy sense of self-esteem. If an eight- or nine-year-old has the capacity to understand the concept of maturity, then the child should have already developed a healthy sense of self-esteem. People with healthy self-esteem don't put other people down to try to build themselves up; they support each other. So by teasing a classmate about being immature, this kid was displaying his own immaturity by demonstrating that he didn't possess the self-esteem of a healthy, emotionally mature three-year-old.

Similarly, adults with low self-esteem tend to operate from the principle, "I am better than you" or "I am the best" (trying to prove their worth); they put other people down in order to build themselves up.

On the other hand, people with high self-worth celebrate other people's successes and operate from the principle, "You're awesome, just like me. You can do it!"

Low self-worth is the most pervasive and potentially the most destructive problem facing our society today. The perception of worth affects how we respond in relationships and how we co-create the dynamics in our relationships, and it even shapes our culture. When we hold the core beliefs of *I am not okay*, or *I am not good enough*, we inevitably try to prove our worthiness or hide our true selves in shame.

When we try to prove our worthiness, we simultaneously sabotage the perception of worthiness by making decisions that confirm our core belief of unworthiness. Basically, in this instance, we adopt one of four attitudes: "I am right and you are wrong," "I am better than you (which makes me worthy)," "If I follow the rules, then I'll be worthy," or "If you think I am worthy, then I'll actually be worthy." All four are attempts to avoid feeling our fear about our worth. Let's briefly look at what's behind these attitudes.

Certainty: University of Houston research professor Brené Brown, Ph.D., author of *The Gifts of Imperfection: Let Go of Who You Think You're Supposed to Be and Embrace Who You Are*, teaches that one of the ways we numb vulnerability is by trying to be *certain*. We all think we are right and we all think, of course, that the way we do things is the best way. The problem comes when we don't respond acceptingly and lovingly to others who do not share our beliefs and when we do not support those around us. If we have a healthy sense of worth, we can allow other people to have a different opinion, making us open to learning new things because we are not trying to protect our worth.

I am so great: If I am feeling small (unworthy), I then have a need to feel big (worthy), and one way for me to get there is to make it seem as though I am better than you. If I only feel an inch big and I can make you feel smaller than me, then I will feel big in comparison. This is a horrible way to feel better about you, and it has a horrible effect on a relationship, yet it happens every day!

Tolerance: If we *cannot* tolerate beliefs different from our own and we need the people around us to agree with us, the real issue is not the content of our beliefs—it's our worth. When we know our true worth, we don't need to be right in other people's eyes. We aren't threatened by differing views; we listen curiously so we can understand more about different beliefs and most of all, we honor other people in our interactions.

If we tolerate beliefs different from our own, listening cooperatively to other people and acknowledging that none of us has *all* the answers, then we can create different relationships and a different cultural environment because we will begin connecting more deeply. It is only then that we can begin to truly resolve differences and create lasting peace, not only in our relationships, but also in religious and political matters as well.

None of us wants to feel vulnerable to the prospect of being unworthy, so we create adaptations to avoid feeling or being seen by others as unworthy. Making deep, authentic contact is one of the biggest factors in healing self-worth issues. Ironically, it is the vulnerability necessary to connect deeply with another person that we avoid when we are scared of feeling or being seen as unworthy.

Appearing strong: Let me share a story that perfectly illustrates this idea. I was driving home late one night from a weekend retreat and was tired, hungry, and needed some protein. I stopped for an egg-white cheesesteak omelet at a Waffle House. I sat at the counter, where the waitress was washing dishes below the counter in front of me. As I ate, she told me about the struggles in her life.

The Department of Children's Services (DCS) had recently taken her kids away after someone had reported her for child neglect. What struck me was her attitude. It was typical victim talk. She complained about the system, she blamed her caseworker, she justified her behavior by complaining that she *couldn't* do what they wanted her to do to get her kids back. She repeatedly said, "It's not my fault! I can't help it if . . ." Then she began to tell me how she was going to sue the state to get custody of her kids back and "make them pay for what they had done."

I asked her if she was allowed to have visits with her kids, to which she responded, "I told them I wasn't gonna do it! They told me that the only way I was gonna see my kids is if we had supervised visits, and I told them that if they didn't trust me with my own kids then I wasn't going to see them at all. I am just going to sue them and get my kids back!" (Imagine me trying not to drop my forehead into my palm and shake my head.)

This young waitress was doing her best *not* to feel unworthy. In the absence of genuine confidence, she was settling for projecting an air of confidence. She talked with arrogance about how DCS had wronged her and deserved to pay, insinuating that she was in the right.

When given the opportunity to have supervised visits with her children, she was so averse to the perceived insult that she could not be trusted with her kids that she refused to see them at all. She was more threatened by the thought of someone seeing her as a bad parent than she was committed to having the best possible relationships with her children. She was willing to sacrifice her relationships with her kids in order to maintain her attitude and show of strength. The tragedy is that her attitude, while it made her feel strong in light of her hidden insecurities, was leading her in the opposite direction from getting her kids back.

I told her that I had worked for DCS and the most important thing her case worker and the judge would want to see is that she was willing and able to comply with the protocols that they had laid out. I told her that there wasn't a judge in the state who would even hear her case if DCS was reporting that she was non-compliant with her treatment plan.

"It truly is their sandbox; you have to play by their rules," I told her. "If they see that you are showing respect for their rules, you will probably get your kids back. At this point, it doesn't matter if they want you to stand on your head and gargle peanut butter. If you want to have your kids back home, you need to stand on your head and start gargling." If she knew her true worth, she wouldn't need to be concerned with her show of strength and she would be willing to do whatever DCS wanted her to do to get her kids back, no matter how it made her look.

While this seems like an extreme case, people in relationships have arguments every day that are variations on this theme. One man described his fights with his wife as "not being about self-worth," but about his "place in the relationship." He said, "I just want to know I am important and appreciated." As soon as he said it, he looked at me, smiled, and said, "That's the same thing isn't it?" When we do not feel worthy, we have to try to get approval or confirmation from others in some way. How many times have you had an argument when all you really wanted was recognition instead of feeling unappreciated?

The most common way that "Am I okay?" issues affect all relationships is when someone cannot tolerate his or her partner saying something that may paint the person in a bad light. This is most apparent when one person gets hurt by something the other has said and feels like he or she is being labeled as a bad person. In projecting or "proving" our worthiness, we break genuine contact by putting our desired image between us and the other person or we attack others in an effort to feel "more than." As

Brené Brown says, "The one thing that keeps us out of connection is our fear that we are not worthy of connection."

YOUR INTRINSIC VALUE

You are a worthwhile person. You were born worthy and you will never be anything but worthy. You have no choice in the matter. The only choice you have is to believe the truth about yourself (that you are worthy) or to believe a lie (that you are unworthy). How would your life be different if you had always believed in yourself and if every time you came upon a challenge, you never feared failing? Instead, what if you knew you would either succeed or learn valuable lessons that would lead to your eventual success—and either way you were okay? What if every time you got into an argument with a loved one, you knew it would end up with the other person affirming you, adoring you for who you are, and strengthening the relationship?

As an infant, you came into this world with no opinion of yourself. You learned one opinion of your worth through your childhood experiences between the ages of 18 months and 3 years. That opinion *may* or *may not* have been the truth. Did you grow up knowing you are wonderful? If you did, you were taught the truth. Did you get the message that you are flawed, not good enough, not worthy, or that you have to prove yourself? If so, you were taught a lie!

Few of us can remember ever being told, "You are not good enough." Yet many of us clearly have this belief. Without a clear memory of being told that we are worthless, we assume that our feelings of worthlessness must come from the core of who we are and cannot be changed. We learned our opinion of our worth more from the *tone* of what was said and from what words were left *unsaid* than of anything that actually *was* said. The good news is that now, by learning the process of how we formed our beliefs about our worth, we can develop the awareness we need to pick out the truth from the lies in the messages we hear from others—not to mention in how we talk to ourselves.

The process by which we learn our opinion of our worthiness is incredibly simple—yet deeply profound in the degree to which it pervades our awareness and shapes our experience. The learning happens at the subconscious level when the neural pathways governing our perception of worthiness are forming from 18 months to three years of age. The bad news is that when low self-worth goes unchecked, it erodes the possibility for authenticity, deep connection with others, genuine introspection, and personal responsibility. Without these things, we shy away from conversations that we fear may lead to our being "proven" worthless or we pre-empt the conversation with an assault of *certainty* or a justification of our feelings so we can avoid being vulnerable.

SEPARATION OF WORTH AND BEHAVIOR

Our culture says that *only* through our behavior do we *earn* our worthiness and that acceptable behavior ensures we will be seen as *acceptable* and *lovable*. This idea is engrained in us between the ages of about 18 months to age three, a period commonly referred to as the "terrible twos." During this stage, children get into everything! They will pull every tissue out of an entire box of tissues, turn plants over, pull books off the shelves and tear pages out, break CDs and DVDs, pop keys off the keyboard, empty dressers and pile the clothes on the floor, crunch food into the carpet, pick the cat up by the tail or hit it with a toy, and pull the sheets off the mattress—and that is just a quick list I came up with off the top of my head. If you have kids, you can probably rattle off another nine or ten examples of your own, just as quickly.

When children are doing all of these things, they are exploring! It is their job! They are not being bad; they are simply discovering their world. That curiosity and sense of adventure is a wonderful thing! Children soon learn what behaviors are "good" and "bad" by what mom and dad like and don't like.

At the same time, their developing brains are forming an answer to the question, "Am I okay?" Our task as parents is to teach them good behavior from bad while *simultaneously* and constantly affirming their worth in the process. Through learning these boundaries of safety and social acceptability *while* developing a healthy sense of self-worth, children grow into adulthood respecting rules, laws, and norms, while all the time believing in themselves and growing into the greatest possible version of themselves.

We have to affirm children's worth not only in our words, but also in our whole demeanor. To teach kids that they are acceptable, we have to accept them—even when they draw on the kitchen table with magic markers! In order to accept kids, we have to accept ourselves. We cannot teach kids that they are wonderful if we do not know our own wonderfulness. If we can't accept the part of us that makes messes, then we won't be able to accept our kids when they make messes, too. In fact, a good practice is to notice whenever we get frustrated with a child, what part of ourselves is it that we cannot accept? What part of ourselves that we don't like is the child reflecting back to us like a mirror?

It never hurts to tell someone that you care, how much they mean to you, or that they are awesome, especially children. So many people shame each other and their kids in an attempt to get them to change their behavior. Shaming people, putting them down, or being cold to those you love may get them to change their behavior, but it does so at the cost of making a closer connection in the relationship.

By separating worth from behavior (in other words, making it clear that the deed may not be okay, but the person is still okay), we can feel our love for one another, communicate that love and acceptance, and still address the behaviors and issues we need to address. When did we decide that it is okay to sacrifice another's self-esteem or the closeness of our relationship in order to have an orderly life?

As parents, we all get tired and frustrated; we all worry for the safety of our kids and we all get triggered by their behavior at times. It's okay, we don't have to be perfect parents. If you do a really good job 80 percent of the time, your kids will turn out great.

Just yesterday, my seven-year-old son shoved my five-year-old daughter from behind after she had wrestled a big sheet of bubble wrap away from him. She fell down and almost hit her head on the corner of a wall. I instantly got angry, even though I saw that she was not hurt. When my son saw the look on my face, he started profusely apologizing to his sister (he really is a sweet kid). I picked him up and put him on the couch and asked angrily, "How many times have I told you *not* to push your sister?"

"I don't know," he answered, trying to wipe his tears away before they could fall.

Realizing that I had not responded lovingly or kindly, I took a breath. I calmed my voice and said, "You are a great brother and a great kid, and it is not okay to push your sister like that." I apologized to him for getting angry and then asked, "When Daddy gets mad, it feels like you are a really bad kid, doesn't it?"

He exploded in tears, nodded his head, and said, "Yes, I am sorry Daddy."

I felt like such a jerk. I hated that I had gotten so angry, and I hated that my son was hurting because he felt like he had disappointed me. I hugged him, held him while he cried, apologized again, told him how much I love him, and told him that he is still awesome, even when Daddy gets mad.

I wish that I had not gotten triggered by him shoving his sister. I wish I had seen that my daughter was not hurt and addressed my son calmly, saying compassionately, "Dude, I *love* that you guys love playing together, and it is not okay to shove your sister. I know you hate losing, and you should be happy for her that she won the fight for the bubble wrap—and then try harder to wrestle it back from her! You're an awesome kid and you still have to go to your room for pushing your sister." My son is not a bad kid; he is awesome. Shoving his sister is *not* awesome. It is important that he knows that *both* are true!

Later that night, I was telling my wife what happened. "You're a good daddy and it's not okay for you to beat yourself up for getting mad," she said, giving me a refreshing dose of my own medicine.

We all can present a laundry list of things that we wish we had not done. Often we believe those things are evidence that we are not wonderful, worthwhile people. We assume that because we have done "bad" things (or didn't do things that we feel we should have done), our worth is diminished. This is simply *not* true. Our worth is not dependent on our behavior. One thing that *is* true is that whether we believe we are worthy or unworthy, we will create that impression in the circumstances of our lives.

It Is Not Okay to Be Okay

If you got the message that you are anything less than awesome, the message may have been reinforced later in life with the warning that you better *not* think you are awesome, lest you be conceited. In the South we say, "Don't get the big head," which means, "Don't let your success go to your head." Both sayings insinuate that you should not think highly of yourself when you achieve any degree of success. The lesson I hear when people confront their worth is even darker than that. People would never say it this way, but their actions and responses clearly indicate that they believe they *have* to think they are worthless or it *must* mean they are conceited and probably selfish.

Arrogant, conceited, and selfish people do exist in the world. Arrogance, conceit, and selfishness are the result of having low self-esteem, not the result of knowing one's true worth. This is a big lesson to learn. *It is okay to be okay.* When people know their own wonderfulness, they also know others' wonderfulness; they do not become conceited. Acting conceited and arrogant are simply ways of avoiding the vulnerability of authentic contact.

Genuine Self-Worth Is Freedom

When you know your own worth, you are free from anyone else's opinion of you. You don't need to defend your worth or your image, and you don't need to try to control what others think of you. How would your life be different if every time someone had said something demeaning, you had laughed because you saw the clear paradox between their message of unworthiness and the truth about your worth? Imagine if you had used the exchange as a launching pad to engage the other person on a deeper level. How would that feel?

Jackie and Darrell came into my office because they had been having issues about finances. She got frustrated with him because she had a money management system that worked really well for her, and he didn't follow her system. He hid money, hid his spending, and repeatedly ran up secret credit card bills. She complained that he continuously set them back when they were supposed to be saving money for their wedding.

When the two of them came in, she spoke as if she were tattling on him. I felt like she was trying to convince me that he was bad and that she wanted me to convince him that she was right. She went on for ten minutes about all the things that he did wrong with money and finances. I interrupted her to check in with Darrell. He said that he didn't have much to say.

"How do you feel when you hear her saying all this stuff about you?" I persisted.

"I've heard it all before, man. It's nothing new."

"I'm sure. This sounds like an old argument, as if it has gone on for years. But what goes on inside you when Jackie starts talking about you like this?"

"Oh man, I just try not to listen 'cause she gets on a roll and she don't stop."

"See!" Jackie interjected. "He don't listen! He just said it. He just wants to keep goin' through life not listenin' to nobody! How's he supposed to quit messin' up if he won't listen?"

Darrell looked at me half pleading, half laughing, as if to ask, "*Do you see what I am dealing with?*"

"When she gets going like this, do you feel like a screw up?" I asked.

Darrell dropped his head and started wagging his finger at me while he looked at the floor. "Awww, man," he responded. "You just said somethin' right there. I been feelin' that way my whole life. That's all

I ever heard my *whole* life. I been feelin' like a screw up as long as I can remember. It ain't nothin' new."

"That's cause you keep screwing up, Darrell!" Jackie interrupted. "I keep tellin' you that you aren't a screw up but you just have to go and do somethin' stupid again." At this point, Darrell started getting defensive and they started bickering. The argument quickly went from, "I am right. You are wrong," to "You are not right, because of [thus-and-such]."

Darrell and Jackie each had a different version of self-worth issues. Jackie acted as if her money management system was the only acceptable way to handle their finances and that anything else was wrong. This type of thinking leads to being judgmental. When she talks to Darrell from this judgmental place, her message comes across to him as, "You are not good enough."

None of us wants to hear that we aren't good enough, and we will either shut down or fight against it, regardless of what the other person is saying. Jackie's financial responsibility was commendable *and* the way she communicated her desire for financial peace in their relationship was destructive to their connection. Her judgmental attitude can be summarized as, "I am okay only if I stick to my financial plan," because she judged herself harshly for her lack of financial responsibility in the past, and she felt that her financial discipline was what kept her from being a mess now.

When she began talking about the "right way" to do things, I began to wonder, *Why is this so important to her? Why is financial responsibility such a dire straight?* I realized she was coming from a place of unworthiness whereby she had to constantly prove her worth through financial responsibility and financial independence.

Because Darrell felt like a screw up his whole life, his feelings of worthlessness had led him to hide money because he felt ashamed (not worthy) of wanting material things. "I wanted a big screen plasma TV," he explained. "I knew she wouldn't go for it, so I hid the money until I could buy it and then I brought it home. I didn't care how she reacted once I got it home." He admitted that he could not afford the television but he felt really good buying it, acknowledging that it was a type of "retail therapy." Darrell was spending money as a way of making himself feel good. In this case it came down to, "If I can have a big screen plasma TV, I won't be a nobody. I'll be somebody better."

The arguments between Jackie and Darrell were a perfect storm for more conflict. He spent money to feel worthy. His spending threatened her sense of worthiness because it threatened their financial security.

She shamed him the same way she internally shamed herself, which contributed to, but was not the sole source of, him seeking more expensive toys to feel good about himself—and so the cycle continued.

Through the course of therapy, Darrell began to realize that he was not worthless. As he matured emotionally, he found himself wanting to mature financially, too. He shifted his focus to supporting their mutual financial goals rather than undermining those goals with his fanciful desires. As he began to make this shift, he started responding differently when Jackie began shaming him with the "you are doing it wrong" message. He began to confront her about shaming and to address the financial issue as a separate matter.

"Sweetie," he would say, "I agree that I should never have gotten those secret credit cards. If fact, I agree with you on *everything* when it comes to money. I don't argue because you are wrong. I argue with you because I hate the way you talk to me about my screw-ups. Whenever you talk to me like I am a screw up, it's gonna lead to a big fight and I don't wanna fight."

When you know you are worthy, you will not feel like your worth is at stake and you can respond more compassionately and more patiently. When you're having a difference of opinion and you feel as though you are being judged or pushed away, you can confront the other person about the shaming message you are receiving and separate the shaming from the content of the disagreement, just like Darrell did. Knowing your true worthiness makes it easier to set appropriate boundaries because you will not feel belittled or buy into another's judgment of you.

So often, I hear stories from people who put up with unfair treatment because they don't feel they have a right to confront the other person about how they are being spoken to because the other person is right about the content of the message. When someone is shamed or attacked about a legitimate issue, two matters need to be addressed: the subject of the attack and the shaming of the attack.

I Am Okay and I Screwed Up

My bank returned a check to me from a client, and when I called her to tell her about it, she was embarrassed. She told me that she would talk to her husband, who paid her monthly therapy bill, and she'd get back to me. An hour later, I answered my phone and heard a man on the other end of the line jovially ask, "How many idiots have you talked to today?" I said that it had been a slow day for idiots so far. "Well, go ahead and mark my name on the idiot ledger because I did something stupid and I am calling to fix it," he responded. I was laughing to myself, totally disarmed, and wondering who this guy was. He then identified himself as my client's husband and explained that he had grabbed the wrong checkbook when he paid me for the previous month. He had paid me from an account that had recently been closed. He apologized, thanked me for all the changes he had seen in his wife, and offered to pay any bank fees that I had accrued.

His self-confidence came through when he jokingly calling himself an idiot. He knew it was a simple mistake and he wanted to make it right. It was refreshing. If he had been embarrassed and tried to make an excuse, it would have felt insincere. Because he knew that his mistake did not affect his worth, we were able to have a more genuine and authentic interaction.

Feedback Is Not an Attack

People with low self-esteem have trouble receiving feedback because everything feels like an attack on their worth and on their character. Conversely, those with high self-esteem welcome feedback because they know that anything they can learn will make their lives better. If I am screwing up in some way, I need help. I need to learn a better way to do whatever it is that I am doing.

If you constantly feel like you are being attacked, let that be an indicator that the problem is probably not that everyone is attacking you. You probably have a pretty low opinion of yourself and you infuse every message you hear with your own belief of inferiority. We have all been attacked at some point; we have all received belittling feedback. We have all been in toxic environments at times where there is no affirmation to be found and putting others down seems to be the lifeblood of the social consciousness. That being said, if this is your *only* experience of the world, you need to heal the self-worth issues that are either keeping you stuck in feeling attacked, hiding in shame, or mired in such a toxic environment.

The crux of this practice falls on the old adage, "People don't care how much you know until they know how much you care." You can find posters displayed in schools and daycare centers everywhere that offer "101 Ways to Praise a Child." This is usually a great place to start, and most of the sayings on those posters are equally effective with adults as they are with children. The key is to find something good to comment on when also addressing behavior that needs to be corrected.

The same is true of working with teenagers, by the way. The goal is to engage them in a manner that helps them eventually begin to discipline themselves, take pride in what they do, and strive not only for approval from others, but also for self-satisfaction about doing good things in their lives. You can achieve this by giving them the respect you want them to have for themselves while still addressing their behavior in an affirming way.

When teens begin to have the respect for themselves that we have for them, then they no longer act immature or defiant. They begin to take age-appropriate responsibility for themselves and make choices in their best interest. By addressing the teens as respectable young people along with addressing their behavior, we begin to see them making better choices because they are no longer working from a negative self-image.

BRYAN'S STORY: THE NO-WOMAN DIET

Bryan Bayer, co-founder of the Authentic Man Program in San Francisco and genuine badass, tells the story of how he began to develop his own sense of worth and presence separate from how others saw him. Bryan realized he was constantly looking for affirmation from women. He had the chance to ask one woman for some genuine feedback after she had turned him down. She took a moment and thought about how she felt with him and said, "I feel like you want something from me. I feel that I have to protect myself from you." Bryan was very clear that he absolutely *did* want something from her. He wanted her to *want* to have sex with him.

Bryan recognized that sex was an indicator for him of his worth. So he took bold action to quit putting this kind of disingenuous, needy pressure on his relationships—he went on a diet. Bryan put himself on what he called his No-Woman Diet! He asked himself, *What if no woman ever again found me sexually attractive? Could I still, even then, be completely in love with my life?* He began loving his life for what it was, not for the affirmation he could get from women.

Inspired by Bryan's brilliance, I developed the No-Approval Diet as a life practice. Here's how it works:

1. Notice when you want approval or begin fearing disapproval from someone.
2. When in that situation, walk away from the interaction! If you are in a meeting at work or some other place where you can't

simply walk away, stop any affirmation-seeking behavior and notice how you feel when you are not getting the approval you want.

3. Make a note of what you want to hear or don't want to hear. Write down the desired approval message using that person's voice. Keep a journal of these messages for a few weeks.

4. Look for common themes in what you want to hear as well as in what you do *not* want to hear.

5. Using these statements, make a list of the qualities you want people to see in you. State the qualities in the positive. For example, if you want people to see you as someone who does not lie, then the quality to list would be *truthful* instead of *not a liar*. This list will accurately describe the person you want to be.

6. Take each of these qualities you want to embody and create an action plan for how to cultivate those qualities in your life.

This practice will take you from a place of seeking the approval of others to approving of yourself and being able to feel your genuine worthy presence in any interaction. If you are taking consistent action in accordance with the person you really want to be, you will begin to see yourself as that type of person, and your self-confidence will skyrocket! You will be satisfied with your own opinion of yourself instead of being dependent on anyone else's opinion of your worth. This practice is not one you can finish in a few weeks; it takes months. If you spend months honing your awareness of the ways in which you don't believe in yourself and constantly cultivate the qualities in yourself that you want to have, you will *know* that you are worthy. You will not shy away from feedback, and you will command attention and respect.

IF WE ARE ALL GOOD, WHY DO PEOPLE DO BAD THINGS?

If everyone is, at their core, innately good, why would people do bad things? The answer is that on some level, their hearts are shut down or they have unhealed hurt or anger inside them. As you begin to get closer to someone like that, the first thing you see is the person's hurt. The way some people deal with their hurt is to act like jerks. Whenever you see an angry person, instead of thinking, *Man, what a jerk*, try instead thinking, *Wow, that person's really hurting*. That person doesn't feel safe enough to share his or her pain, only the anger. Set appropriate boundaries to keep yourself safe and hold the space for the other person to heal by saying a prayer affirming the person's goodness. When we as a people are able to shift our awareness away from being afraid that we're not enough into knowing we have the right to set boundaries and to not tolerate inappropriate treatment, our communities will begin to shift in a drastically powerful way.

This brings up the question, how do you communicate when somebody's doing something you don't care for without judging the other person? The best way is to use the word "and." With my son, ideally, I would say, "You are so wonderful. I love that you're so curious about the world, *and* it's not okay to stick your fingers in the electrical outlet." Or "You are such a wonderful big brother, you're so creative, *and* it's not okay to put your sister in the oven." After taking one of my workshops, a participant posted this status on Facebook: "You are such wonderful children, *and* it's not okay to lock Mommy's keys in the car." It's the same with adults, except that we are not responsible for teaching adults social acceptability.

Relationships take on a different tone when we are constantly affirmed—by ourselves and others. We can receive feedback more easily, and we can be open to hearing another person's feelings about problems in the relationship. When we know our true worth, we can drop the need to be right and get to the true roots of the conflict. That in turn allows us to feel accepted, knowing we belong, and we can enjoy the closeness we share with the one we love.

PRACTICES:

- When you disagree with someone, say to yourself as though you were talking to the other person, *I am certain that I am right AND I want to hear more about where you are coming from.* Don't make it your goal to change the other person's mind; make it your goal to understand why this person believes what he or she believes.
- Whenever you feel as though someone is putting you down, ask yourself if this other person doesn't like you or if he or she doesn't like your behavior. Ask, "Is it me you don't like? Or is it what I am doing that you don't like?" If the person is more inclined to accept responsibility for his or her own feelings, you could ask, "Are you upset with me? Or do you just not like how you are feeling?"

- When you make a mistake, tell someone that you made a mistake and affirm your own worth in the confession. Say, "Even though I am awesome, I made a mistake."
- Ask for help whenever you need it.
- Whenever someone else is angry, frame his or her anger in your mind as pain, and then see the hurt underneath the pain.

CHAPTER 7

SAYING "NO"

I sat in a group of about 75 people who had gathered to hear a Native American medicine man named Joseph Rael speak. At the end of his talk, he took questions. A woman sitting in the front row asked, "Grandpa Joseph, I have had this sinus thing for years now. I have constant congestion. I am always stopped up and my nose runs. What is going on with that?"

"It comes from the place of saying 'yes,'" he answered. The woman looked at him, confused, waiting for more clarity. We were all confused. I was wondering if he had really heard her question.

"Maybe there are some places in your life where you need to say 'no,'" he added. A hushed and knowing, "Ooooooohhhh…" went across the room. Everyone recognized that we *all* have places in our lives where we say "yes" to things when we really want to (and probably ought to) say "no." Women stereotypically are taught to say "yes" when they want to say "no." Men are just as bad about doing things we don't want to do and making decisions that don't reflect who we truly are, we just do it differently.

Setting boundaries is one of the most important skills we can ever learn in creating awesome relationships. Most of us were taught to *not* set boundaries (and our parents and others modeled not setting them) in order to avoid the emotional outburst or hurt feelings that may result. Therefore, few of us have skill at setting, enforcing, and feeling at ease with boundaries.

The truth is that sometimes we have to say "no." Saying "no" allows us to stay in integrity. In order to more fully say "yes" to what we want and who we are, we must be able to say "no" to what we don't want and who we are not. Setting boundaries protects us from harm and gives us the space to be who we truly are.

I am constantly amazed at the lengths some people will go to in order to avoid setting a boundary. In fact, the prospect of setting boundaries brings up so much anxiety for some people that it's one of the most common reasons clients drop out of therapy. They simply don't want to deal with it; instead, they hope the situation will just get better on its own. Most often, these are the same people who find themselves in relationships where they feel unappreciated, taken advantage of, and dismissed.

Let me share a good example of why we all need to set boundaries. When we're in a heated argument, being honest and real (being authentic) with the other person makes us vulnerable. Many of us see vulnerability as a weakness because experience has taught us that when we're vulnerable, we get hurt. This does not mean that vulnerability is bad, though. It means that the other person is not being vulnerable, is not being emotionally responsible, and does not recognize and value authenticity—and it means that we need to draw strong boundaries with that person (and sometimes with ourselves about what we will and will not tolerate).

We have to be able to say "no" in any relationship. Being able to say "no" to people and things that are not good for us gives us the safety and freedom to say "yes" and drop deeper into emotional intimacy with people who *are* good for us. When we don't feel emotionally safe in a relationship or when we feel as if a part of us is not welcome, we don't feel safe to bring all of who we are. Then we can't really be authentic, which as we've discussed previously is part of walking a path of enlightenment and is the foundation of awesome relationships.

Two common types of situations call for us to set boundaries. One is when we feel like someone is violating our space in some way; in that case, setting a boundary is necessary to remain emotionally or physically safe. The second situation, which is more innocent but can be just as powerful, is when we are letting someone know how we feel. All emotional sharing is not boundary setting, but sometimes sharing how we feel with someone can be a wonderful, disarming way of letting the other person know that we are not satisfied with what is going on or with what is *not* going on in a relationship.

WHAT GETS IN THE WAY

The most common reasons people give for *not* setting and enforcing boundaries are that they don't want to be mean, they don't want to be the bad guy, they don't want to upset anyone or hurt anyone's feelings, they're afraid of being alone and don't want the other person to go away, or they think the other person wouldn't be okay with that boundary. While these are all valid concerns, they do not keep us safe and certainly don't give us the necessary emotional safety to drop deeper into a close, intimate relationship. So let me debunk each of these statements, one at a time.

"I don't want to be mean." Selma's boyfriend had been verbally abusive for the last several months of their relationship, ultimately ending in a physical altercation that brought her into therapy. She had grown up with a mother who was mentally ill and could rarely be held accountable for her behavior. Her father had been mostly absent. Selma concluded that having a relationship with a guy who had what she called a "strong" personality felt like a welcome relief from the chaos and turmoil she had always known growing up with her mother. At 21 years old, she hadn't been out of her parents' home for very long.

While doing a boundary exercise in my office, Selma took a long rope that I had given her and marked out a part of the room to represent her space. She took a few moments to move around in her space and take a few breaths. She said it felt freeing to have her own space.

I warned her first, and then I got right up to the line and pretended that I was about to step across the line. After having the toe of my boot hovering over the line for a few seconds, as if I were going to violate her space, I asked, "What do you wanna say right now?"

Selma looked away, and then looked back at where her boundary was about to be violated. She looked away again, then at my boot again. "Oh my Gaaaaawd!" she exclaimed, visibly frustrated. "Men are such bastards!"

"That's true." I responded. "We *are* bastards. And if we are not going to pay attention to your boundaries and have the integrity to stay on our side of the line, *you* are going to have to set us straight." I pointed at the boot threatening to violate her boundary. "How do you feel right now?" I said. "And what do you want to say?"

"Back up?" Selma asked very quietly and sweetly, as if she were asking me if it was okay instead of just telling me what she wanted. It was a great first step towards setting firm boundaries. I stepped back to where I was clearly behind the line.

"Good job. I was about to violate your space and you told me to back up," I said. "Way to go! In just a second, I am going to do it again."

"Nooooooooooooo," she whined. "I feel like I am being so mean."

"There is nothing mean about setting appropriate boundaries," I responded. "You have to set boundaries to keep you safe at all times. When someone is violating a boundary with you, *that person* is the one who is being mean. It is not okay for someone to violate you or your space. If someone is violating your boundaries, the responsibility to keep you safe is with *you*. It is unreasonable to expect someone who is a big enough jerk to violate your boundaries to take good care of you. *You* have to take good care of you." Selma nodded, seeming to understand.

I stepped back up to my previous spot and began hovering my boot over her line again. "Now this time, don't say it like a question," I instructed. "I want you to look me in the eye and say it like you mean it."

After several tries, Selma found her voice, looked me in the eye, and firmly said, "Back the f*#k up, or I am gonna hurt you!" My blood went cold; I knew she was serious. She turned around and shook her arms to release the tension and added, "That's exactly what I should have said to Shit-head about three months into the relationship."

Selma wouldn't have been mean if she had said this to her boyfriend, who was forevermore referred to as "Shit-head." She would have been keeping meanness *out* of her relationship. If we do not do this with someone who has a tendency to be mean, then we are essentially saying that the meanness that he or she perpetrates is acceptable. A relationship with healthy boundaries is much, much more fun!

"I don't want to be the bad guy." Wendy had been stalked for nearly a year and told me that she didn't feel safe anywhere. In her trauma, she had no sense of personal space and felt like it was not okay to set boundaries. When I proposed a phrase to use with a co-worker who regularly came into her cubicle and sat on her desk to talk, she said that she didn't want to be the "bad guy."

"Are cops *bad guys* when they arrest someone committing a crime?" I asked her. "Maybe they are to the criminals. Police officers are there to keep the bad guys from perpetrating harm onto others, just like boundaries."

"Yeah," Wendy said, getting angry. "Well the cops didn't do a damn thing when this jerk was terrorizing me."

"Yeah, I know." I replied. "And I am sorry. That's not how it is supposed to work. The cops are supposed to take care of problems so we don't have to. But hear me say this: If someone came through that door right now with intent to hurt you, I'd f*#king kill them! I would. And I wouldn't lose a bit of sleep over it. Does that make me a 'bad guy'?"

"No," Wendy answered.

"You are safe here," I told her. "In this office, I will destroy anything that tries to hurt you."

Wendy sighed and visibly relaxed. "Okay," she said. "I believe you. I do."

In this case, I was the one setting the boundary and demonstrating that it is okay to set the boundary. Setting healthy boundaries is not bad. Setting healthy boundaries makes us bad people only in the eyes of the people who want to violate our boundaries.

"I don't want to upset anyone or hurt anyone's feelings." Better them than you, I say. When you set boundaries, you take a chance on someone being hurt or the relationship not getting as deep as it could. The good news is that by setting boundaries, you are actually preventing future chronic pain and opening the door for deepening emotional intimacy. By *not* setting the boundary, on the other hand, you may be allowing a relationship pattern to be established that could be the source of recurring hurt and/or frustration.

My good friend Carolyn Buttram, who is a counselor, stand-up comedian, teacher, and eternal wise ass, says, "The truth never hurts anyone." I amended her statement slightly: the truth never hurts anyone, even when it stings like a bitch! The truth can sometimes be a bitter pill to swallow.

No matter how bad the hurt, when you accept the truth, you are one step closer to enlightenment. It is okay to tell the truth even if it is going to hurt someone's feelings. When the person is important to you, let the other person know how much you care and how important he or she is to you as part of the boundary setting (as we discussed in the last chapter). Chances are that the person needs to hear it or that *you* need to say it—either way, you are bringing the relationship more into alignment with the truth because you are being authentic.

When you know that sharing the truth is going to sting the other person and you have to share in order to get closer, remember that you are not the one who is bringing the pain into the other person's life. That pain was already there. You are simply uncovering it by trying to get closer (Bright Lights Cast Dark Shadows).

"I am afraid of being alone and I don't want the other person to go away." This is a big one because it uncovers two very important possibilities. First, the people who feel this way may have a fear of abandonment— an increasingly pervasive issue in our society that is separate from the issue of boundaries and which needs special attention to be healed. Often when someone has a strong fear of abandonment, he or she will avoid setting a boundary even when no actual threat of the other person going away exits. This is another example of Hurt Feelings Are Like Rowdy Teenagers, whereby people keep subconsciously creating situations that mirror a buried hurt.

If fear of abandonment is holding you back from dropping deeper into emotional intimacy, set boundaries that challenge your fear and put you back on a path of faith! Fear and love cannot exist in the same space, so if you constantly cater to the fear by not setting boundaries, you are actively disallowing love from coming into your life.

The second possibility can be another bitter pill to swallow. If someone is acting in such a way that warrants your setting boundaries and is refusing to honor the boundaries that you set—and if setting a boundary may actually trigger him or her to leave—then your life may be better off without that person. If your boundaries are not welcome in the relationship, it means that part of you is not welcome, which means it may be time to re-evaluate the relationship. Lack of boundaries or resistance to boundary setting means fear is running the show, not love. Ending a relationship is a big deal and I don't mean to dismiss how hard the ending of a relationship is. My hope for all relationships is for both partners to heal the hurts that get in the way of the relationship being awesome. Sometimes that means making big changes, which the other person may see as your "changing the rules."

One friend described the nature of his marriage this way: "I chase her. If she ever stopped running, it would throw me off. I would say, 'What are you doing? That's not what we do. Go! Run away! I'll come get you.'" While my friend was describing their playful game of chase and catch, he also shared how he never doubted for a second the connection they shared and how they stop the game when they need to connect to solve a problem.

So often, one person in the relationship is relatively happy with the way things are (or at least happy being unhappy), while the other person is not happy. The happy one usually doesn't want things to change and will often resist change to varying degrees.

If someone in your life is not open to having the deeper relationship and better life together that setting boundaries would provide, then that partner could possibly become an anchor that you would have to drag around on your life's path—a constant source of hurt or frustration. I often say to a client, "Just because you love the person doesn't mean he (or she) is any damn good for you." We all want our lovers to love us so much that they would walk through the fire of their own pain in order to be with us—but not everyone is willing to do that. The good news is that when you share how you feel without blaming the other person, take responsibility for your part in creating the current situation, and tell the other person what you want, you've made an excellent start toward making the shift necessary to create an awesome relationship.

"He (or she) wouldn't be okay with that." I hear this or some variation of it when someone wants to avoid another person's angry outburst as a result of a boundary being set. We rarely like having people set boundaries with us. It usually causes us to look at a part of ourselves we would rather not see, or the boundary prevents us from getting something we want right away. With this in mind, it is easy to see how an angry reaction is simply a type of temper tantrum. In that situation, we must be willing to weather the emotional storm that may result from our healthy boundary setting. In fact, we can even set *additional* boundaries to keep us safe from the other person's reaction to our initial boundary setting.

During the course of therapy, Chelsea decided that she needed to set a boundary with her mother around her mother yelling at her over the phone. The mother and daughter would talk on the phone at least four to five times a week, and sometimes every day. While Chelsea loved her mother and *wanted* to talk to her nearly every day, she also felt an impending sense of doom whenever she got on the phone with her. She decided that she would not stay on the phone if her mother began raging at her during the call.

While talking on the phone three days later, Chelsea's mother began yelling at her, so Chelsea hung up. She immediately sent me a text message to celebrate her victory. "I did it," she messaged. "I hung up on her when she started yelling. I felt so rude hanging up on her, but my whole body relaxed when I did."

When Chelsea came in for her next appointment, she shared, "I waited until the next day to call her. Waiting was hard, but I did. I apologized for hanging up, and I asked her if she wanted to finish our conversation. She started yelling again. So I hung up again and called her the next day." Chelsea went on to tell how she hung up on her mother for six straight days. She hung up every time her mother began yelling at her over the phone. After the third day, Chelsea felt comfortable telling her mother what she was doing.

"She didn't like it," she told me, "but she said that she wished she hadn't listened to my dad when he had yelled at her for all those years. So I think she understood." I asked Chelsea how she had told her mom that she would continue to enforce this boundary.

"Mom, I love you," she told me she had said, "and I love talking to you right up to the point when you start yelling at me. When you yell, I don't enjoy talking to you anymore. Whenever you yell at me, I am going to stop listening by getting off the phone. It's not because I don't love you and it's not because I don't want to hear what you have to say. It is because I don't want to hear you yell."

Telling her mom what she was doing did *not* stop this life-long pattern immediately. Eventually, by Chelsea's maintaining this boundary, the boundary became unnecessary and mother and daughter began sharing in a deeper way with more vulnerability. The mother eventually shared that she always figured it was okay to yell, because yelling was so commonplace in both her family growing up and also in her marriage. Chelsea was able to share with her mother how much she loved her and how she enjoyed being close to her—and in so doing, she separated her mother's worth from her mother's behavior. By setting a boundary, maintaining that boundary, and affirming how much she loved and valued her mother, Chelsea took steps to allow her and her mother to slowly deepen their relationship, shedding years of hurt and angst.

N. M. F. P. (Not My Problem)

Possibly the most destructive aspect of the boundary issue is not setting boundaries with yourself about what you take on from others and feel responsible for what truly is their responsibility. When people get triggered by your behavior and you have clearly done nothing wrong, you could offer them the gift of letting them heal the trigger (if they are open to that) by allowing them to suffer through the mess they have made and learn their own lessons. You may have heard this referred to as tough love. You can still remain compassionate and listen, and you can support others in their struggles, while at the same time not assuming that their feelings are your responsibility. Loving the ones you love, however, is *always* your responsibility.

One couple I counseled spent almost every waking hour together because Jan became really anxious whenever she left Matthew alone. She was scared of him going to bed before her and of him getting up before her, and when she'd return from an errand, she'd act aggravated with him because she was so scared of what he might have done when he was alone.

In therapy one day, he was discussing how his lack of exercise and sleep hindered his productivity. So he set up a daily schedule for himself and went over it with me. "But that won't work," he suddenly said, taking a closer look at his plan. "I can't go to bed at 9:00 every night because Jan doesn't always go to bed at the same time."

"Sure you can," I responded.

"But she gets upset if I go to bed without her," he replied. "Am I just supposed to go to bed even though it upsets her?"

"Underneath her fear and anxiety, what she wants more than anything is for you to be the greatest man you can be," I told him, in front of her. "Taking good care of yourself is a crucial part of being the best man you can be."

Being well versed in therapy with me, Jan replied, "N.M.F.P. Or in this case, N.Y.F.P., sweetie. I won't like it *and* I don't want you to *not* take care of yourself."

"How about if you give her the gift of feeling her own feelings?" I asked Matthew. "What you are doing now is pre-empting the blow up you are afraid of." Boundaries aren't a weapon. They're about doing what you can to be fully present in the relationship. In this case, Matthew needed to set two boundaries—both of them within himself. He needed to go to bed on time, and he needed to not take on his partner's anxiety about being separated from him, instead deciding that Jan's anxiety did not mean that he couldn't take care of himself.

While Matthew was growing up, his mother was prone to daily fits of rage, sometimes several times a day. He and his siblings could never predict or control their mother's outbursts, so they simply tried to keep their mother from getting triggered. Matthew was not able to say, "Mom, I know you are upset and I did not do anything wrong." Saying this probably would not have curbed his mother's behavior and may even have enraged her further, but having developed this skill at a young age would have prevented Matthew from carrying this fear of another person's rage into his adult romantic relationships.

As a result, Matthew lived with the fear of having a woman be angry with him and never challenged his assumption that it was his responsibility to always "make women happy." When he quit taking responsibility for Jan's emotional state and began challenging his own fear of her anger, he was able to set healthier boundaries with his sweetheart and respond more authentically and more compassionately when she got scared.

TAKE THE INITIATIVE

Shania was a single mother whose daughter was in kindergarten. The daughter's best friend and soccer teammate had a father who wanted to date Shania. He had never directly asked Shania out, but he constantly suggested that they do things that would have them spending more time together. Shania didn't mind the girls playing together, but she was repulsed when this man was around. He wouldn't leave her alone. He sent her text messages, he constantly tried to help her out with babysitting by offering to schedule play dates for their daughters, and he even offered to fix her toilet once when she had been talking about household projects.

"I can't blame him because he doesn't know how I really feel about him," she complained to me, "but he keeps trying to get in my space and I don't want him there. He's not a bad guy; I just don't want him in my space."

"Say 'no,'" I suggested. "Tell him how you really feel about him."

"Well, he hasn't ever asked me out on a real date. So I haven't ever had the chance to say 'no,'" she responded.

"*Make* the chance to say 'no,'" I said. "This guy probably won't ever give you that chance. On some level, he may well know how you really feel about him, so he will not create a clear chance to be shot down. Instead, he is going to keep trying to weasel his way deeper into your life. How about if you say, 'Dude, you are a good guy and I love that our daughters are so close. I want to be clear with you. I feel like you are always trying to get deeper into my life. I need you to hear me say, 'I will never go out with you.'"

"So you want me to be cruel?" she asked.

"No," I responded. "I want you to be firm with the guy. I don't want you to feel like a prisoner whenever you are in the same room with him. It sounds like it sucks to be around him."

"It totally sucks to be around him!" she said. "I guess I have just been hoping that he would eventually 'get it' and quit following me around like a puppy."

Shania was complaining about this guy getting in her space, and as Chapter 5 discussed, complaining is a clue that the person feels stuck in the victim mindset. Victims feel powerless. If you do not want to feel powerless in a relationship, set boundaries, enforce those boundaries, and begin demanding what you want. Quit settling for what others give you and then being silently unhappy with it.

SETTING BOUNDARIES IS NOT ENOUGH; YOU MUST ACTUALLY ENFORCE THEM

"I only have to be willing to get up one more time than him," Deena said about disciplining her son. Her son tested limits with her all day, every day. She recalled all the times when she prayed to have the strength to not give in; no matter how tired she was. She prayed, "God, help me remember that I am investing in my child's future by not letting him break the rules, even when I am *this* tired. Help me remember that if I let him get by with everything he tries to get by with, I will be infinitely more tired in his teenage years because I will be up all night worrying about him every time he goes out." She knew that boundaries had to be enforced consistently to be effective.

Through her constant efforts, Deena's son was able to slowly learn to channel his massive energy into more productive things than testing boundaries and breaking rules. He began excelling at sports and music, eventually landing a spot in the city's youth orchestra.

In his bestselling book, *Social Intelligence: The New Science of Human Relationships*, Daniel Goleman, Ph.D., writes, "Lack of boundary setting with children leads them to have a sense of entitlement and the inability to delay gratification." This applies to adult relationships, too. If someone is taking advantage of you in some way, you are not setting boundaries. By not setting boundaries for equality or appreciation, you are opening the door for other people to feel *entitled* to whatever they get from you.

When boundaries are set once and not enforced—or when they are not enforced consistently—the boundary is fairly useless and the setting of the boundary is a waste of time and energy. Setting a boundary one time is not enough to effect change. The boundary must be set and enforced.

Sometimes when I suggest that a client set a boundary, the client will respond, "I said that. It didn't change anything," or "Boundary setting doesn't work with my husband." These statements are simply the voice of frustration; either the client did not set boundaries in an effective way, or he or she did not enforce the boundaries with appropriate consequences.

Our ways of interacting in relationships are largely habit, so when we want to establish a new habit, it will take time and we will go through a learning curve in adapting to the new way of being. Without consistent reminders, we won't be able to establish the new habit as thoroughly as we want (or possibly at all).

Thomas was an entrepreneur whose business ventures kept him busy much of the time. Even so, on most days he was able to stop work and connect with his wife Susan for a little while, usually several times a day. Susan's main way of dealing with stress was to complain, and she was always stressed. Thomas loved Susan dearly, and he often felt that her complaining (and the emotional guardedness that went with it) kept her from being present and so kept them from being as close as he wanted them to be.

"I provide very well for us financially, but sometimes I start to resent her spending habits," he shared, his expression showing obvious frustration. "It's really not about the money, I know that. It's cool having more money than we can reasonably spend and I kind of like it that she has so much fun with all our money. I just start feeling like she doesn't care about me, and that comes out initially as my resenting her spending habits."

For Thomas, feeling resentful is an indicator that he is not feeling fulfilled in his relationship. Describing Susan as "not showing up in the relationship," he wants her to be more emotionally available. Several times in the past when he has mentioned his frustration, she has apologized, agreed that her complaining was her way of dealing with stress, and let him know that she didn't want to push him away. "She would always make an effort to be closer for a couple of days, maybe even for a week," he said, "and then something would come up and she would be gone again."

Neither of them reported feeling a lack of time together. Thomas simply wanted more connection and playfulness with his wife. Ideally, the habits people develop reflect genuine feelings. In this case, Susan's complaining didn't reflect her feelings for Thomas; instead, her disconnect reflected her frustration in her own life. He came into therapy to get some guidance on the situation.

"How often have you let her know how frustrated you are?" I asked.

"I know it brings up some really big stuff for her so I only bring it up once in a while, maybe three or four times a year," he said. I asked Thomas how often it bothered him.

"Every day!" he exclaimed. "You are not suggesting I should say something to her every day, are you?"

"What would that be like for you?" I asked.

"I don't want to be a nag," he responded. "You know, you hear stories about people, usually women, who are unhappy and all they do is nag their husband. I don't want to be like that. I don't want to be another source of stress in her day. So I don't know what to do."

I asked Thomas how he handled problems in his business life. Then I asked, "How would your 'business brain' handle a problem like this?"

"Oh man, that is simple," he said with ease. "Our mission is to give people what they need better than they thought they wanted it. I would tell an employee how we do things and then keep an eye on the person, coaching them and encouraging them to always keep excellent service in the front of their minds."

"So what would you like your wife to have in the front of her mind?" I asked.

Thomas looked really sad and said, "I want Susan to be as excited to see me as I am to see her. I mean, I know she wants to see me, but she doesn't show it. I can't feel it. Does that make me needy?"

"How about if every time you feel her being distant, you tell Susan how you are feeling?" I offered.

"She will just take it as criticism, like I am telling her that she is not enough," he lamented. "If she weren't enough I wouldn't want to be so close to her."

"So, tell her that. Susan needs to hear how good she feels to you, and she needs to hear how excited you are to get closer to her."

"I do. I tell her all the time," he said.

"Do you tell her how you feel right at the moment when you feel her disengage?" I asked.

"Dude, I would be jumping on her all the time,"Thomas said laughing.

"Well, I wouldn't suggest jumping on her. Maybe more of a loving, compassionate, and caring approach would be more effective," I said sarcastically. "She might not even be aware of what she's doing, or she might not be aware that you are so frustrated."

"So how do I tell her?" he asked.

"You love her like crazy!" I said. "That's the first step: feel your love; feel your passion. Both when you are with Susan and when you are not with her, feel how much you love her." I described the visualization practice detailed in Chapter 4 and suggested he do that as a first step, practicing it 20 times a day.

"The second step is expressing it," I continued. "Let yourself get excited as you tell Susan how you feel. Tell her how excited you get about her and how much you want to feel her excitement, too. Step three is the tricky one. While still feeling your love for her, tell Susan every time when you feel let down or sad because you want her to engage with you more than she's currently doing."

"But how do I say it?"Thomas wanted to know.

"You could simply say, 'Right now I am feeling frustrated.' Or maybe develop a code word or phrase that you've both agreed on to indicate that. It could be as simple as 'distance.' The important part is to share the vulnerable emotion: 'I just got sad, because I want to feel you more.' The key is to find something that works for both of you," I explained.

"Like 'comforter,'" he suggested. "She has said at times that she thinks love should feel like a big, overstuffed down comforter of joy wrapping you up. I want her to wrap me up in her love. . . 'Comforter.' That's what I always try to do with her."

Thomas was using sharing his feelings as a way of setting boundaries with Susan. He wasn't saying, "You have to do *this* or *that* will happen," as with Chelsea telling me to back up or I would get hurt. Instead, Thomas was saying, "I want more of you than I am getting. I want our relationship to be better."

When Susan came to therapy with Thomas several weeks after the "comforter" conversation, she quickly settled in and seemed at ease. "Marcus, it's good to meet you," she told me, "and I don't know whether to hug you or kick you in the head. The last three weeks have turned my world upside down."

"How so?" I asked.

"Thomas told me about everything you guys have talked about and he has been watching me like a hawk. I have had people telling me my whole life what I am doing wrong in relationships—that people like me and I shut them out, that I don't let anyone care about me, that I am so smart and I should do more with it, or that I can do such amazing things and I should make something of myself. I don't want any of that. I just want to live my life," she said, sounding frustrated, and with just a hint of making fun of herself.

"And here I am telling him to ask more from you," I interjected.

"*Yeah!* You big jerk!" she threw out sarcastically.

"I'm such a bastard," I said, matching Susan's sarcasm. "How dare I talk him into trying to get close to the woman he is absolutely crazy about? I apologize. Intimacy is wrong. Love is wrong. I should re-think my whole life."

"Maybe you should, you big jerk!" she said with an insincere pout. Thomas was smiling, adoring her.

Continuing to play along, I asked, "What would you have him do with all those feelings of wanting to be close to you, adoring you, and feeling disappointed when you won't let him close to you?"

"Oh, God. I don't know. Just tell him to stop," Susan said, beginning to tear up.

"I hear you," I responded. "Thomas is shaking things up and you don't like it. And here's the problem: I have known you for only about five minutes and I can already tell that you are one of the coolest and most charismatic women I have ever met. He's known it since the moment he met you and he is still goofy over you."

"Yeah, that's the part that's messin' with me," she said. "All my life I have protected myself against criticism, against people telling me I am not good enough. He's not criticizing me. I keep bracing for it and I still freeze up, you know, waiting for the other shoe to drop. He's doing it because he wants me and because he cares. I have to drop my guard to let him close, and that's scary."

"It *is* scary," I replied. "Any time we make ourselves vulnerable, we take a risk."

"Thank you!" she exclaimed. Turning to her husband, Susan added, "See, you are scaring the crap outta me!"

"I am trying to *love* the *fear* out of you," Thomas responded.

"Yeah, I know," Susan said. "And it makes me nervous. How do I know you aren't gonna blast me if I let you in? I mean, I know you won't. I'm just scared." She began to tear up again.

"I know, sweetie," Thomas told his wife. "I know you are scared and I am not going away and I don't want to hurt you. Really, all I want is to love you. I want to feel you as big as I love you. 'Cause I love you *that* much." Hearing Thomas's words, Susan softened.

I interrupted, saying to her, "Now look Thomas in the eye and very lovingly say, 'If you hurt me when I am vulnerable, I am gonna kick your ass!'" Susan smiled and tuned to her husband with a shy look, tears still in her eyes.

"If you hurt me," she said, her smile turning from shy to playful, "I am gonna f*#king kill you. Do you understand me? I will *f*#king kill you*."

Thomas never broke eye contact as Susan spoke, never stopped smiling at her, and never stopped feeling his adoration for her. "Deal," he told her. "I completely understand."

Thomas used his feeling of frustration to guide him in communicating when he wanted more emotional intimacy with his wife. It wasn't that he felt less of Susan. Quite the contrary! He was feeling frustrated because his expectations of living a life where he felt wild excitement and passion for his wife were not being met, partly because he hadn't expressed those expectations clearly to her. And Thomas wasn't willing to compromise on that expectation. He was committed to enforcing this boundary whenever he felt Susan was being distant. He remained vigilant in bringing his passion to his wife's attention with gentleness and compassion until her icy shell had melted away.

We have to be able to say "no" in order to create the emotional safety we need. When we set appropriate boundaries, we prevent unhealthy situations from forming. This not only keeps pain out of our lives, it creates a space for healthy, authentic interactions to take place and it allows us to be more who we truly are in our relationships.

PRACTICES:

- If you have trouble saying "no," find a partner and take turns asking each other ridiculous questions and making outrageous demands of each other. (For example: "I want you to go buy me a camel!" "Will you go build me a space shuttle?" or "If you don't paint the state of Rhode Island pink, then you don't love me.") Come up with the most outlandish things you can think of and give each other the chance to practice saying "no."

- Do the above exercise again, and this time practice feeling loving compassion for the other person as you say "no." When the person makes an outlandish request, say, "I love you and I am not going to do that." Maintain eye contact as you breathe deeply and exhale a blessing breath of love onto your partner.

- Identify one toxic relationship in your life, and then cut it off. Give yourself permission to stop having contact with someone who brings you down. Make room in your life energetically for a positive person who supports and nurtures you.

- Tell someone how you feel when he or she does something hurtful. As part of setting this boundary, explain that you care about the other person and want to be closer, and that is why you are telling him or her that what this other person did or said hurt you.

CHAPTER 8

SAYING "YES"

In the "Q Who?" episode of the television show *Star Trek: The Next Generation*, a character named Q says of exploring outer space, "If you can't take a little bloody nose, maybe you ought to go back home and crawl under your bed. It's not safe out here. It's *wondrous*, with treasures to satiate desires both subtle and gross. But it is not for the timid." Q could have just as easily been talking about love and authentic connection in relationships. Love is not safe from the potential of hurt. Opening one's heart to another always involves risk. Does that mean we should stay closed and isolated?

Let's say we're talking about investing money. Would you rather hide your money under your mattress and earn no interest at all, put it in a secure CD at a 2 percent yield, give it to a local stock broker to earn the average 5 to 10 percent annual return, or get training in how to invest money from the masters who consistently get 20 to 30 percent or more, year after year?

Aiming for larger gains financially brings greater risk, that's true. Sometimes, investors experience large swings that can be scary. However, some people know how to consistently earn huge returns on their investments. They acknowledge the risks and very rarely suffer the losing side of the deal. When they do lose large amounts of money, they typically make it all back very quickly!

How do they do that? They are financial masters in their particular disciplines. They do not give way to fearful thinking in the face of risk because they have confidence in their skills to handle tough situations without losing money. They keep safety measures in place to protect what they have, and they know that if they do lose money, those same skills that earned them money in the first place are exactly what they need to earn it all back again. They trade with confidence!

Making authentic connections in a relationship is the emotional equivalent of consistently earning 20 to 30 percent returns on your investments. There is risk—of being hurt or let down. The reward, however, is feeling as if God has put an angel on Earth just for you, one who will support you and whom you can enjoy.

The only reasons we avoid opening to emotional risks are either ignorance (we simply don't know how because we have never been taught) or fear (we fear pain because we have not healed pain from our past). When we haven't healed old pain and still carry it, the risk of more pain feels unbearable.

In relationships, couples have to be willing to risk authenticity in order to have really rich, healthy relationships. There's no guarantee of return—no assurance that being authentic is going to land well with the other person or that he or she is not going to use what is shared to emotionally beat up the person sharing. But without taking that risk, couples end up being very guarded with each other.

Rest assured that with the ability to set and enforce firm, clear boundaries, you will be able to create your own emotional safety just like the financial masters create financial safety when making risky trades. For example, my wife and I both hate conflict, yet we are not scared of it. Instead, we delight in the sharing and closeness that resolves the conflict. Our disagreements never turn into fights because we create a loving space for each other to get in touch with the pain or fear that is going on at a deeper level. When that pain is healed, it won't get in the way of a loving connection anymore. It is a pretty incredible feeling to know that we probably will never have one of those knock-down, drag-out fights, ever! Some couples feel like they are having a good week if they only have one of those. Good for them! We should all celebrate every success along the path to wholeness, and only fighting once per week cannot compare to healing the closed places that lead to those fights and feeling the connection that brought you both together in the first place!

We have to say "yes" to closeness in order to engage in a deeper, more authentic way. We have to say "yes" to the intensity of creating more emotional connection through becoming present. As we learned in Chapter 1, feeling the intensity of our feelings is the path to healing and also to getting the closeness we want—which is especially true with making emotional connections. Making a genuine heart-to-heart connection is the foundation of intimacy. In order to take our relationships to a higher level and cultivate deeper closeness, we have to become comfortable with connecting with each other deeply.

When we say "yes" to getting closer to our beloved, it also includes becoming closer to ourselves (as we learned in Chapter 2). We are agreeing to feel all of our own feelings that may come up when we begin to get closer to another (Bright Lights Cast Dark Shadows). It also means saying "yes" to what we may feel when the other person becomes fully present and begins to share more of who he or she is. It means saying "yes" to the fear that may come up when we get triggered by another's sharing, committing to *feeling* it and not *reacting* to it in an effort to protect ourselves. The most profound and sometimes the most challenging part of saying "yes" is being adored and accepted by a person whom we adore and accept.

BECOMING PRESENT

The first step in making such a deep connection is becoming present. There are two ways to accomplish that: You can go up on a mountain and sit in a cave for 30 years until you become enlightened, or you can take a breath. Either way works. Here's the catch: Taking a breath doesn't mean simply moving air into and out of your lungs. We all have been doing that since birth, and few of us have become enlightened. When I ask you to take a breath, I am asking you to check in with your whole being. Feel your physical body. Feel your emotional body. Feel where you have tension. Feel where you are relaxed. Notice how it feels to be *you*, right this second. Notice the thoughts going through your mind. If your emotional heart had a voice right now, what would it say? How about your gut? Do you feel any tightness in your throat? Where is your energy level at this very second? How about now? How about *now?* These are just a few of the important pieces of awareness.

Presence is becoming aware of everything that is going on in our entire being in the moment. When we become aware of who we are *in this precise moment*, we are present. The most common hurdle to becoming present for many people in our culture seems to be emotional awareness. Without feeling our feelings, we are not capable of being present, being authentic, or making a deep emotional connection.

After taking a breath and becoming aware of what we are feeling in the present moment, it is time to take another breath, refresh our awareness, and feel what we are feeling in the next moment. After doing work with clients around focusing their awareness on their breath and cultivating awareness of their feelings, I will say as they are walking out the door, "Take a breath, feel what it feels like to be you, and repeat that every six seconds until I see you next week." Making relationships awesome requires our presence—not just some of the time, *all* of the time!

<h2 style="text-align:center">AUTHENTICITY</h2>

The second step in making deep connection is authenticity. On one level, that's making what is coming out of our mouths match what's going on inside. The key is to feel our feelings and then to share them in such a way that the other person can hear them.

Authenticity through vulnerability is a vital part of the path to increasing emotional closeness. Without authenticity, there's no true resolution when problems come up. When most couples have an argument, they fight, then they quit fighting, and then they ignore the fight to some degree as they try to get back to the good feelings that are possible together. While it's good to feel those good feelings, that does not resolve the issue. Unresolved issues ultimately lead to more distance, hurt, and mistrust. Most couples try to ignore the fight because they simply don't have the tools to be able to resolve their internal conflicts or the conflicts they have with each other. So all that really happens is that they shut down. The solution is to develop their mindset, emotional skills, and communication skills so that they are able to tolerate the uncomfortable feelings of deeper vulnerability, allowing true resolution to the problems they face together with their partners.

Authenticity for men: Working with men, I often trick them into being more authentic and having better relationships by telling them it will lead to more sex with their wives and girlfriends. While this is often true, men quickly love the feeling of being authentic and making deep emotional connections with a woman, and wanting more sex quickly takes a back seat to experiencing authenticity itself.

The key for men is to realize that when they are authentic, women experience them as being safe and trustworthy. This is based on the principle that women are like tuning forks for what's going on with men emotionally. Women's emotional radars are tuned in just such a way that they are able to sense men's emotional states. This is roughly where the term "women's intuition" comes from. Women may or may not interpret a man's emotion 100 percent accurately because their own emotional state can skew their perception, yet for the most part, women have a better sense of what is going on with their men than the men do themselves.

Women will sense when men are angry, they will sense when men are happy, and they will sense the discord when men are saying one thing and feeling another. Women have this sense in part to keep themselves safe, so they can sense danger. Men and women alike have the potential to have and enhance this intuitive sense as they do more of their own healing work. In essence, the better they know themselves and leave nothing hidden from themselves, the more they see and feel in others.

If I'm feeling insecure, and what comes out of my mouth is very boastful, people will not perceive me as trustworthy or emotionally safe. If I'm feeling angry and I stay in my head (as many men do), sharing only what I am thinking, then my words will not match my buried emotions and my wife is not going to feel as if she can trust me or what I am saying.

If men want their women to feel safe with them and trust them, then they have to get in touch with what is going on inside of them, especially the feelings that they would rather ignore and pretend are not a part of them. Once they get in touch with those feelings, they have to be able to communicate them in an appropriate way.

Authenticity for women: Women may have the harder job when it comes to authenticity and making emotional connections. Having the intuitive sense of what is going on with others adds an extra responsibility of being clear to their work. When women cannot clearly distinguish the boundary between their own feelings and another's feelings, then every hurt they sense in another person will feel like their own pain. The antidote for this problem is to know their own issues; they don't have to heal them all, but they do need to be aware of them.

Be willing to feel your own pain and know it so well that you can distinguish every nuance of it, so when you feel another's pain you will be able to identify what *is* your own pain and what is *not* your own pain. When you sense someone's pain and can clearly define the boundary between your feelings and the other person's feelings, you can respond with empathy, compassion, and love instead of reacting in fear as you might if you felt the pain as your own.

A woman can model authenticity for a man by feeling her own feelings and inviting her man to feel his. She can honor her own voice by sharing her feelings without apology, accepting her man and his feelings when he does the same, and thanking him for sharing how he feels. He will feel the difference in her when she shares that she's frustrated and that she still accepts him.

When she is frustrated, and she shares it, her man will feel the difference between her accepting responsibility for her own part in creating her frustration and her nagging him because she doesn't like what he's doing. He will learn to feel the difference in her being present and her pulling away from him. He'll feel the difference if she says, "I love you so much, and I'm really frustrated right now. I wanted to get a lot of cleaning done tonight. I didn't tell you that I wanted you to help with the cleaning this evening. I am not saying you have to do it. I want you to know how frustrated I am that you didn't do what I wanted you to do, even though I didn't tell you what I was wanting." In sharing her frustrations this way, she takes responsibility for her own feelings and makes it clear to her man that he is not responsible for her frustration.

Awesome relationships require couples to be transparent in a way, and that transparency requires them to be vulnerable with each other. In the example above, the woman is making transparent that her frustration comes from her own desire for her man to do more around the house. In sharing that it is her desire that is causing the frustration, her confrontation will land much differently than if she spoke to him saying, "You need to do more around the house." By avoiding this common pitfall, which can sound like an accusation, the floor is now open for a more genuine discussion about what she wants.

What Am I Saying "Yes" To?

We can't know what we are saying yes to when we begin to make genuine deep connections with another person because it is the very nature of such deep connections to be spontaneous and creative. We never know what is going to happen when we engage with the heart of another. We don't know what another person feels until he or she feels it and shares it. We don't know how the other will react or how our genuine presence will affect him or her. We also don't know how the other person's presence will affect us. So we can't ever be certain what will happen as we embark on this emotional journey of authenticity. The experience of getting close to another person is truly an unknown.

What we *do* know is how we feel when we're around the other person. We know the excitement we have felt up to this point as we have gotten closer. And with practice, we will know we can set appropriate boundaries to keep ourselves safe. The task is to stay open because there is no greater support, affirmation, or love that can happen than when we are open with someone we love. Further, by understanding how each relationship is unique, we can begin to understand the type of awareness that fosters being present in our intimate relationships.

Because each relationship with each person is different, the experience of being in each person's presence will be unique to being with that person. A lot of people try to put relationships into boxes. "Oh, that's my cousin so this is how we get along," they may think. Or "This is how a boyfriend should be," "Husbands should do _____," or "I want my friends to be there for me." That puts limitations on the relationship.

While having a friend "be there for you" is a wonderful thing, you may have struck up a relationship with a friend who cannot be there in the way you want. Expecting that will only create strife. Unless you communicate what your expectation is and you're open to not getting what you want, you are setting yourself up for feeling let down. In essence, you are saying the relationship has to be a certain way instead of allowing it to be exactly what it is.

Whenever you put limitations on how a relationship can be, then you're not allowing all of what it is capable of being. Ultimately, you are not allowing yourself to be who you truly are, or allowing the other person to be who he or she truly is. Often you may get what you want, but you won't get it how you thought you were going to get it. If you are attached to *how* you get it, then you may end up disappointed, and then you miss out on the gift of getting what you needed in the way that God had planned for you.

So many clients tell me that they are afraid that if they give up what they want in a relationship, then they will never get it. I give them this guarantee: If they accept their relationship as it is, it will feel better than if they try to make it into what they want it to be.

I am not saying you should give up what you want with your partner. Part of connecting deeply with another person is sharing how you feel, which includes what you want. Indeed, share how you feel, and stay open to your want not matching what the other person can give. You might just find that what you want is far smaller than the potential the relationship has to offer. Accepting the relationship as it is may feel to your partner as if you are accepting him or her, which may be the invitation to fully show up that he or she has been secretly wanting from you all along. The only way to know is to breathe and experience the relationship as it unfolds and to share how you are feeling.

So why do we create intimacy? We do it to be closer to God, to feel our own energy, to feel the love from another, to enjoy how incredible we feel when we bring more and more of who we really are into the world, to enjoy *all* of what life has to offer us, to feel the creation energy as we heal ourselves and help facilitate the healing of others through our presence, and most of all to play!

If playing and having fun is just not your thing and you want to make your relationship empty, dull, predictable, and boring, then *don't* make authentic emotional connections. Such connections are exciting and dynamic. Once you make such a connection and feel the healing presence of God in a relationship, there is no turning back. So if excitement is not for you, then you need to learn the following tricks to keep your heart and awareness shut down. The psychological term for the ways we avoid genuine heart-to-heart connection is "contact boundary disturbances," but I prefer to think of them as Relationship Death Accelerators.

RELATIONSHIP DEATH ACCELERATORS—HOW NOT TO BE PRESENT

If you think making deep connections will bring up too much for you and you aren't sure you can handle it, I suggest beginning to master the seven Relationship Death Accelerators, outlined below.

Deflection: Deflection is avoiding awareness or making a deeper connection with your beloved by not expressing yourself directly or by not receiving what the other is trying to give. Two of the most common ways that we deflect are to change the subject and to only share what we *think* instead of what we *feel* in the moment. Tense conversations take on a whole different tone when we stay with an uncomfortable subject and let go of our thoughts, which are usually arguments about who is right. When we breathe deeper into our feelings, allowing ourselves to feel our vulnerability and sharing our feelings from that vulnerable place, tense conversations transform.

Tina and Tom had been married for six years. Tina was a successful business owner; Tom was a highly trained Navy SEAL. Tina complained that she and Tom could not communicate about *anything*. When Tom spoke, he never shared his feelings; instead he shared a formulated argument that usually took the form of pointed questions geared towards proving his point. Often his thoughts were about what *Tina* could do differently, with Tom never feeling his own feelings much less allowing himself to feel vulnerable.

"I know he loves me," Tina said in therapy. "I have never doubted that, but I often feel he is not really capable of love because he is so cold."

"I asked her to tell me what *she* was willing to do to change things, to make things better," Tom responded. "She wouldn't answer me. She just walked away." His response ignored Tina's request for warmth. While complaining is never a good way to get what you want, Tina was crying out to feel connected to her husband and neither of them had the skills to recognize and facilitate making the connection. Instead of getting in touch with his own warmth and speaking from that place, Tom responded with a cold, tattletale comment that implied that his wife was not willing to work on the relationship. This response was a deflection that came from avoiding his own vulnerability *and* attempting to keep the focus off of him, which further avoids the chance of making connection.

Projection: Projection involves not seeing our own issues clearly, yet accusing someone of doing exactly what we are doing ourselves. This comes from not wanting to acknowledge and take responsibility for our issues, or simply being blind to them, and attributing those issues or behaviors to someone else.

One of the most common projections I hear from women is, "He doesn't support me." While it is often true that the husband or boyfriend does not offer the support that he could, it always comes out in therapy that the woman is not taking good care of herself by supporting and honoring her own desires. The same is true when a woman complains, "He doesn't care about me." It's usually the case that she is not showing herself the care she needs and is blaming her lack of self-care on him.

When we all take the responsibility for taking good care of ourselves, it takes a lot of pressure off of the relationship. We then step into our own power, and our partners are much more likely to support us because they can feel the power of our authentic presence. They may fight against it at first, though, and that is when we have to set boundaries around how they interact with us.

Another projection I often hear from both men and women is, "He's [or she's] not interested in sex." What I usually find is that people who say this don't express all of their own sexual energy with their partners. Instead, they often act disinterested out of fear of being flat-out rejected or fear of being rejected for being too sexually aggressive. This issue can only begin to be resolved when one partner shares his or her frustration with acceptance and compassion and without blaming the partner.

People who repress their own anger will often accuse others of being angry. By blaming their partners for being angry, these people get to avoid taking responsibility for their own anger. If they are not comfortable with anger, then their partners could use projection as a particularly effective tool for keeping the attention away from themselves.

Men also share quite often that they feel unsupported by their partners, saying, "She doesn't back me up." The men who say this usually aren't supporting their partners as well as they could because they secretly feel weak and are trying to cover up their own insecurities. They want their loved ones to constantly build them up so they can avoid feeling their own insecure feelings.

The solution to all of these situations is to allow ourselves to feel our genuine feelings, own that we are the one feeling them, and share them in an appropriate way. Projection happens when we haven't developed the awareness of our own emotions or when we try to hide them, either in general or around a specific issue.

Often, I see a combination of deflection and projection. For example, the husband of a client was having an affair, using late nights at work as his cover for romantic interludes. When his wife confronted him with her suspicion, he started screaming at her: "You have no right to ask me that! I don't know what you are doing all day while I am at work and slaving away to support you and the family! I am working ten, 12, sometimes 16 hours a day, while you are doing God knows what! I don't know who you are with when I am not home! I don't even try to keep up with all the men in your life—your trainers, your so-called doubles partners, that guy you get naked with—that massage guy! I can't believe you would ask me something like that!" In his response, he was deflecting attention away from his behavior while also projecting his own affair onto her by insinuating that *she* couldn't be trusted and might be having an affair herself.

Retroflection: This is doing to ourselves what we *really, really* want to do to someone else. The most common example I see is when people get quiet when they desperately want to tell someone else to shut up! This pattern is set up in infancy, when we learn to handle our emotions. The pattern carries itself into the partners we choose and how we respond to our own feelings.

When people retroflect by getting quiet, they actually have a lot to say. They turn their desire for the other person to be quiet onto themselves, while a quiet storm rages inside. This shutting down often happens when people feel unworthy in some way. Not sharing what they are feeling makes intimacy impossible. It may keep the peace, but they pay for it with the vitality and freshness of the relationship.

Another example of retroflection is when people make a poor decision that keeps them stuck in bad situations, or when they hurt themselves when the real desire is to hurt other people. Hurting themselves or turning their anger inward has devastating effects on their own emotional health and the emotional health of their relationships. When people turn their anger in on themselves over a long period of time, they begin to feel beaten down; everything that doesn't feel good is met with more anger, which is again turned inward. All these layers of anger turned inward causes depression. It is a tragedy that most people who suffer day to day with depression have never had a healthy relationship with anyone who gave them permission to authentically share their feelings, especially when they get angry. As Chapter 5 discussed, the manner in which people deal with emotions is set in infancy, when they also set a template for the people to whom they are drawn.

Introjection: "My mommy is mean and her car is stinky because she smokes in it all the time," said an eight-year-old boy caught in a custody battle. His father had custody and regularly vilified the boy's mother. The boy repeated this statement over and over whenever he wasn't sure what to say during a conversation about his feelings for his mother. In reality, he had really warm feelings for her that were in conflict with the message his father had programmed him to say. In each session, the boy would spend the first 20 to 25 minutes repeating the lines his father had drilled into his head. Then something inside would soften and he would begin sharing how much he missed his mom and how he wished he could see her more. He even mentioned how cool he thought her car was (without mentioning the "stinky" smell).

His father had given the boy a set of beliefs that the boy had taken on as his own without considering whether or not they felt true for him. Introjection is almost like the Jedi mind trick, whereby we are told what to believe and we agree to believe it, without questioning what we are now believing. This gets in the way of making a true connection with another because we are acting from a set of beliefs that may or may not match who we genuinely are, in which case we can only share who we think we should be.

Egotism: When my wife's officemate finished a tense phone call with her mother, she pushed her chair back from her desk. Then she began spinning in the swivel chair and saying, "I am my mother. Look, the whole world revolves around me! The whole world revolves around me! The whole world revolves around me!"

Egotism is a habit of making everything about oneself. People who display egotism will either take everything you say and relate it to a story about themselves or they will ignore what you are talking about and talk about what they think is important, leaving very little room for you in the conversation. People who do this are rarely able to have empathy for others and seem to need quite a bit of attention. This comes from the fear that no one will be there for them so they have to grab all the attention they can. The problem is that their behavior cuts off the possibility of making the genuine connection that they desire because they are not open to appreciating another person for who they are.

Confluence: Confluence in relationships happens when the two people in a couple try to be exactly like each other, not acknowledging any differences between them. While many people believe in the adage, "in marriage, the two shall become one," there's a huge distinction between a couple being seen socially as one entity and the partners themselves believing there is no difference (or boundaries) between them. I often see people who get into relationships and stop doing the things that they like to do and do only the things the new partner likes to do. This comes from a desperate desire to be accepted and to avoid the fear of conflict or the fear of loss. The subconscious belief at work here is, "If I am just like this person, we will never have problems and I will never lose him or her." The problem is that the authentic close connection is lost.

If one person likes to hike and the other person doesn't, it seems like a simple thing to say, "I want to go hiking and I get scared when I think about going without you." Usually just making that statement will bring about a sufficient level of openness to resolve the fear, or else it will bring the fear out into the open so it can be addressed directly instead of avoided entirely. But for confluent couples, even making that statement feels too scary a step to take. Yet it is only when we are separate people that we can experience the excitement of coming together in the relationship. It is the connection in relationships that is exciting, not the dissolving of individuality.

Isolation: When couples completely avoid connecting in an effort to avoid pain that they are afraid of, they're practicing isolation. While isolating can give people a chance to cool off after a fight, and while it also gives those who are loners a chance to recharge their batteries, it can be harmful if taken to an extreme. Even when people isolate temporarily, in an authentic and deep connection, they come back together refreshed and restored.

Genuine connection requires commitment. If we are not committed to diving deeper into our relationships with each other, we will shy away when tough emotions come up or when we have something vulnerable or scary to share. We have all learned ways to avoid vulnerability and deeper connection. It is important to realize that all of that learning has served us in helping to keep us from being hurt further and it has also *not* served us in creating deeper, more meaningful relationships.

PRACTICES:

- Ask your partner to sit across from you. Make eye contact with each other and breathe. Feel how you feel being in each other's presence. Allow a story from the past to pop into your head. What feelings come with that story? Are you scared to share it? It just may be the one story your beloved has been dying to hear from you. Share it.

- Think of something that has frustrated you for a long time. Write down all the ways that you have contributed to the situation being so frustrating. Ask your partner if he or she is willing to hear you share your frustration and ask if he or she is willing to hear you take responsibility for how you have contributed to that frustrating situation. Share all the things you did to contribute as well as what you wish you had done instead. If you wish you hadn't done some of the things you did and you don't know what you could have done differently or are at a genuine loss for what you could have done instead, share that too!

- Remember that deeper connection doesn't require us to be fearless; it requires us to share our fears as a function of authenticity and vulnerability. With that in mind, identify some of your fears and share them with someone close to you. For example, you might say, "I am scared to tell you when I am sad because I am scared you are going to think I am weak. I want you to think I really have it together," or "There are times at work when I feel like a fraud," or "Sometimes when I look at you, I feel like I am going to explode with love and I am scared that if I tell you, you won't feel the same way." Whatever your fears are, *share them!*

CHAPTER 9

TAKE A BREATH

When e-mail first became popular, before the days of social networking, half of the e-mails people sent were forwarded jokes. I still remember one of them; it was a list of answers on a second-grade science test that were so wrong they were funny. One child said, "When you breathe you inspire. When you don't breathe you expire." I was stunned at the simple wisdom conveyed in this answer—to me, this was absolutely no joke! I made a poster of it to put up in the house.

Emotion (e-motion) is energy in motion, and *breath* is the motion. If we don't breathe, then energy gets stuck in our bodies. We can process a lot by talking about our thoughts, although at some point we will need to heal things inside that our thoughts can't access. As I've explained earlier, to keep us from feeling pain, our minds create adaptations—thought patterns that help us avoid becoming aware of buried pain. Fortunately, our bodies still remember the pain, even if our minds have tried to forget. Using breath is one of the easiest and most effective ways to bypass our conscious thoughts and get in touch with our buried emotions so we can finally feel them and heal them.

THE LOWER LUNG BREATH

During my third year of graduate school, I took an intensive yoga class taught by a yoga master named Nataraja Kallio. I thought I was taking an easy elective. I did not realize what transformation lay ahead!

That class changed the way I do therapy, and it changed the way I relate in my personal life. We spent the first month of the class learning and practicing only the lower lung breath. I thought I could breathe pretty well—until the class started. I had years of a solid meditation practice, and this class asked something different of me.

I wasn't getting it. I wasn't getting the breath. I wasn't getting anything. I was doing everything asked of me—holding all the postures, exaggerating my exhale to make room for something fresh and new— but nothing was happening for me.

Then during week three, something shifted. I was lying on my back, my knees bent, and I was breathing. I started feeling a slight static type of feeling in my stomach. I visualized breathing right into that feeling, breathing life into it. My breath dropped down so deep that I could feel the pressure on the inside of my hip bones, and tears started rolling down my face. I immediately started wondering why I was crying, which distracted me from the breathing, and then both the tears and the feeling in my stomach stopped. *Don't think about it, Marcus,* I told myself. *Just breathe.*

I started breathing again, and the feeling came back. The tears returned, too, and they kept coming. I didn't hear much of what was said in class over the next 20 minutes, I just kept breathing. Although the emotional pain was intense, feeling the pain felt better than when I had stopped breathing. That was when I began to see that without the breath, we don't get to experience the deeper reaches of our pain; we deflect.

So why was I crying? About two weeks before the semester started, I lost a horse. He died of West Nile virus. I was out of town at the time, and when I got home, my business had me booked solid until the day classes started. I never had, nor made, a chance to grieve. I had earned a living on this horse's back eight hours a day for nearly two years. At one point, he got really sick, losing 40 percent of his body weight, and I nursed him through an illness from which I didn't think he would recover. And even after all that, a mosquito took him out while I was away at a weekend retreat.

And that's how, three weeks into the semester and five weeks after my horse died, I found myself lying on my yoga mat with tears pouring out of me. I was in touch with my emotional body—finally. After the class ended, I went up to Yogi Nataraja and described what had happened. He just smiled and said, "Good. I wanted you to get this piece." He knew how valuable this awareness was and that I didn't have it before. And I suspect he knew how important this skill would become in my work. He was really excited for me. He is a true teacher and a good friend.

Any clients who have worked with me since that time know that if they're not breathing, they're not feeling. Many times, I ask people to take a breath and share how they're feeling. When they open their mouths and say, "I think…" I stop them right there.

"I don't care what you're thinking!" I tell them. "I'm not interested the least little bit in what's going on in your brain! I care what's going on in your *heart*. If you're telling me what's going on in your brain, you're not feeling what's going on in your heart. Any thinking you do will not have vital information until the breath has awakened the heart. The time for thinking will come later, after the heart has shared its secrets."

No matter how good a thinker you are or how good of a plan you have for what you're going to do, if you heart is conflicted, it will subvert any other plans you may have. As I've said earlier, whenever you have unresolved feelings, those feelings are going to leak out in some way and undermine your efforts (Hurt Feelings Are Like Rowdy Teenagers).

Motivational speaker T. Harv Eker, author of *Secrets of the Millionaire Mind,* does a great job of describing how the subconscious mind will take over our finances when we have subconscious limiting beliefs about money. He refers to these beliefs as "toxic weeds in our financial garden," and describes how they will kill the roots of our financial plans, ideas, and dreams. This is also true emotionally! No matter how good a partner you intend to be, your unresolved pain will constantly prevent you from being everything you can be in your relationship. Because breath can help you access the unresolved pain buried in your subconscious, it can often be the key to healing and wholeness.

WHY I AM A BASTARD

Diane learned just how important breath can be when she came to me for help with an unusual affliction. She shook most all of the time, except when she slept. She had started shaking in high school, although it had been very faint then and no one had noticed. Her shaking had worsened over the years until it reached the point where it was noticeable most of the time. Her doctors couldn't explain it medically and because it was causing massive anxiety, they referred her for therapy.

Diane would sit in my office and complain—about her boss, her kid, her mother, her siblings. The things she complained about had very little to do with her. Every now and then, she would touch on a genuine feeling. Without realizing it, Diane would quit shaking for a second, and then she'd begin telling another story that had little to do with her and nothing to do with how she was feeling at the time. I would feel her leave every time she wasn't present anymore.

Diane had told me bits and pieces of the horrible sexual abuse she experienced at the hands of both her mother and her father. She always talked about it as if she were just mentioning the abuse in passing, as if all the details were common knowledge. She later became aware that talking about her abuse in this way enabled her to acknowledge it without actually feeling the feelings around it. This way, Diane could say to herself, *I didn't hide my abuse from my therapist.* Yet even though she was acknowledging the abuse, she was still deflecting the pain, which prevented her from being present and prevented her from healing the pain.

When Diane felt the feelings around that abuse, she quit shaking and I could feel her presence. Even though she was touching on some very painful emotions, the air around her seemed to grow warmer and I could feel her presence get bigger. One day, she made an offhand comment about her mother coming to "sleep" with her in the morning, which was when the sexual abuse from her mother occurred. I could sense Diane feeling the pain and fear for a few seconds, and then she began telling another disconnected, pointless story. I stopped her, asking her to go back to the feeling she had just had.

"You mean about my mother?" she asked. "What about it?"

"Take a breath and let yourself feel it for a moment," I suggested.

"Oh, no," Diane said, wagging a finger at me. "No, no, no, no, no. We don't do that. I can barely make it through the day as it is. We don't go opening up *that* can of worms. We keep a tight lid on those feelings. You got that, mister?"

"Did you notice that you quit shaking whenever you let yourself feel that hurt?" I asked.

Diane looked shocked. She got it. Her mouth hung open and she was speechless. I could feel her presence again.

"You mean I have to feel that shit or I am going to keep shaking for the rest of my life?" she asked.

"No, I don't think so." I told her. "I think you are going to keep shaking only until your heart and soul give up. Once you decide to just be miserable for the rest of your life, your body will quit trying to get your attention," I said with loving sarcasm.

"You're a bastard, you know that?" Diane responded, matching my sarcasm. "I just want you to know—you're a bastard. Okay, I will take a couple of breaths, but I am not going to promise that I won't punch you."

"Agreed," I said with a smile and a respectful bow of my head.

"Okay, how do we do this. . . this. . . this *torture* thing you are going to put me through?" she asked with her usual deflective, victim-based sarcasm.

"Just breathe," I told her. "Hear the sound of the air going into and out of your body. Feel the air flowing in and out . . ." I continued to walk her through about ten minutes of guided meditation to get her settled into breathing. We ended by visualizing her breath flowing across her heart, on its way to her lower abdomen. By this point, Diane was sobbing.

"If your heart had a voice right now, what would it say?" I asked.

"I just want to disappear so no one can see me," she said. As she felt her emotional pain, she kept breathing. She then recalled a story that explained why she wanted to disappear. She remembered hiding under her bed with a knife at about age 11. She knew her drunken father was going to come into her room, wanting to touch her. This was the most vulnerable I had ever seen Diane. She was stepping into the vulnerability well, and I didn't want to do too much on the first day.

"Stay with that feeling for a few more breaths," I told her, instructing her to take three more big, long, slow breaths. "Now," I continued, "with the next few breaths, I want you to slowly, very slowly, come back to this world. Take your time. Just breathe." Diane took several minutes to slowly come back. Then she wiped her eyes and looked at me.

"That wasn't as scary as I thought," she said. "It still sucked. I don't want to think of myself as a person in that much pain, but I guess if it's in there and I can't ignore it anymore, I may as well get it out, right?"

"Right," I said. "Take a few more easy breaths." We both did this together. "I want you to do something similar to this at home tonight," I continued. "I want you to snuggle up to your husband, either on the couch or when you go to bed. Lay your body against his, feel his strength supporting your weight, and breathe! Feel what it feels like to have your skin touching his skin, feel your breath as you let yourself melt into him. If he asks what you are doing, just say, 'I am going to just lay here and drink you in for a minute.' Can you do that?" Diane nodded while a few final sobs popped out.

"I can do that," she said with warm relief. "I would *really* like that. I haven't been very good at letting myself get close to him lately."

Over the course of the next year, Diane came in almost every week and gave only brief updates on the dramas in her life. Instead of telling empty stories, she would begin breathing, dropping her breath into the deepest reaches of her emotional body. By the end of the year, her dramas had all died off, and she hadn't created new ones. Her visits eventually tapered off until she quit coming in. I got a card from her a few years later that said simply, "Thanks for teaching me to breathe."

DRAMA

If the whole breathing and feeling the pain thing is not for you, you have another option—*drama!* Drama is not nearly as fun in the long term, but it does allow you to avoid any pain buried inside. Drama is the soul's way of trying to create the same emotional intensity as your buried pain, so you get to experience the intensity without actually feeling the pain that you're afraid of. The problem is that all of the effort you put into solving the problems created in your drama doesn't address the real emotional wound that is fueling the drama.

How many people do you know who have a lot of drama in their lives? How much drama do you have in *your* life? If you have a lot of drama, you won't recognize it as drama. It will just feel like *life*. You can't see beyond your own defenses. If you are closed down about something, you won't see beyond the veil that you put in front of your own eyes. The tragedy of drama is that when you are working really hard to put out a fire in a drama you've created, you never get to heal the root hurt that caused you to create the drama in the first place.

I challenge you to ask ten people who know you really well if they see you creating drama in your life. If you think of a few people who you really don't want to ask because you are afraid of their answer, *those* are the people you really need to ask. Push yourself to ask them—but just make sure first that they are people who care about you.

PRESSING PAUSE—AND TAKING ACTION

Taking a breath is like pressing the pause button on life; it allows us to stop the normal noise that keeps us busy in our heads. It allows us to begin slowly opening our awareness to the feelings that are lurking underneath. I use the word "lurking" as a joke, because the feelings we bury inside can feel like sharks waiting to attack us. In reality, those feelings are simply waiting to be felt, but we treat them as if they are monsters out to maul us because that's how they feel—

until we actually begin to feel them.

Every feeling you ignore eventually feels like it grows too big to handle. But rest assured, you are stronger than you think. Just breathe and let yourself feel what comes up. Continue to practice expanding your awareness through your breath. If you pray, take the time to listen after your prayers are finished. Say your prayers, then breathe. Take a walk every day and focus on exhaling fully with each breath. Become part of a community that is dedicated to personal growth and that practices what it preaches. Find a breath coach and do lots of sessions where you learn to cultivate your mind-body-spirit awareness. Find a church that supports mind-body-spirit growth and rejects fear as a coercion tactic for teaching its spiritual message. Visit several yoga studios and find a teacher whose presence and teachings call you to touch the deepest parts of yourself. Find a Holotropic Breathwork workshop. Join a meditation class or attend a regular meditation group. Do something to further your practice of breathing well, so that you can be in deeper contact and experience a deeper connection with yourself.

PRACTICES:

- Practice the physical mechanics of deep breathing. Train your body to easily take deep breaths. Exaggerate your stomach expanding as you breathe in. Exaggerate the exhale, blowing out a little more air than you usually do. If you start to feel light-headed, slow down—you are working too hard. Visualize breathing gentle life into the deeper parts of who you are.

- Think of an interaction you had with someone close to you that became heated. Close your eyes and picture yourself back in that argument. Feel the tension in your body; feel the frustration or the anger you felt. Remember every detail you can about the argument. Your mind may be filled with all of the things you said, could have said, or wish you had said; you may think of the perfect come back.

  Now imagine holding a remote control and pressing the pause button on the whole scene. You don't have to be in a hurry to react anymore. You have nothing to lose by taking a few moments to return to a peaceful, loving place where you feel centered and grounded. Then, check in with your body. Feel the tension in your physical body and also in your emotional heart. Identify how you are feeling. Finish the sentence, "I feel _____."

Ask your heart what it wants to say. Ask your heart what it wants the other person to hear. What do you want in this moment? What are you truly scared of in this moment? Imagine sharing with the other person how you are feeling, what you are scared of, and what you truly want.

- Three times in the next 24 hours, take a breath and check in with your emotional body while you are talking to someone. Finish this sentence in your head, as if you were talking to the other person: *As I am listening to you, I am feeling* _____.

- As you snuggle with your beloved, breathe! Whether you are clothed or not, feel every place your bodies are making contact. Let your awareness seep into those places. Identify how your partner's skin or contact feels to you. Now let yourself feel it again. If you quit feeling it, adjust your body to create fresh contact and breathe. Allow yourself to sink into your beloved and imagine that your get to drink him or her in by breathing through your skin in all the places where your bodies are touching.

CHAPTER 10

RESPONSIBILITY AND BLAME

We must each accept responsibility for ourselves, for our actions, and for our feelings if we want to live awesome lives and have awesome relationships. This involves owning our part in the messes that we have made in those relationships—instead of blaming other people or circumstances, or otherwise deflecting. Whether we are aware of the decisions we make or not, we must realize for the sake of our happiness and growth that we are the creators of our feelings and actions. This includes accepting the fact that our actions affect other people. That is not to say that we *make* other people feel the way they do; it is that our actions help create their environment.

If we don't accept our responsibility for our feelings and actions (which helped create our environment), we are destined to feel stuck and powerless. Certainly things happen to us that are outside of our control, yet it does us no good to complain about them. We need to accept that these things have happened, feel the resulting feelings, and then decide what we need to do in order to make our lives what we want them to be in light of our circumstances, *even when we don't like those circumstances*.

The two biggest ways people avoid accepting responsibility in relationships are playing the role of the victim (thus avoiding owning the power to make changes) and feeling as though they need to defend themselves because of low self-worth. (Sometimes those two situations exist simultaneously, although not all people who feel victimized have low self-worth and not all people with low self-worth think they're being victimized.) Often, when people play the part of the victim to avoid responsibility, what they really want inside is for someone to know how badly they are hurting.

Three behaviors that indicate someone is playing victim or is suffering from low self-worth are complaining, blaming, and justifying—which I'd now like to add to the list of Relationship Death Accelerators (my term for contact boundary disturbances) discussed in Chapter 8. While these are all technically examples of deflection (the first Relationship Death Accelerator), they hold such incredible power to screw up what might otherwise be a great connection that I want to give them special mention.

Complaining: Complaining and its immature sibling whining are voices that say, "My life is horrible," "Poor me; this hurts," "I was done wrong," "Why are you doing this to me?" and "There's nothing I can do about it." All of these boil down to, "I have no power; I am not responsible for being in my situation." Complaining is rampant in society (especially in the workplace), and for some it's a way of life. Yet few things are more destructive to morale than complaining, which has never been an effective means of creating meaningful change.

Blaming: Blaming is all about self-worth. Many people think of this behavior as part of problem solving because when there's a problem, people tend to ask, "Whose fault is it?" Yet blaming doesn't actually solve any problems. When there's trouble in a relationship and you wonder, "Whose fault is it?" there's only one truthful answer: *ours*. We co-create our relationships, even the ones that feel lopsided. Both members of a couple contribute to creating the relationship when it is good, and both are equally responsible when the relationship is horrible.

Of course, when a problem occurs, diagnosing what went wrong and identifying the exact moment when feelings got hurt can be very helpful. Understanding how current problems are created and learning the needed lessons from those problems can help prevent future problems. The important part is feeling and not deflecting those hurt feelings so we can communicate authentically from that hurt place.

When people feel unworthy, they respond to others blaming them as if the blaming threatens their worth. Not surprisingly, making blaming statements can escalate a conflict quickly. People try to dismiss the validity of what the blamer is saying in an effort to dismiss the blame. Dismissing a blaming statement feels to the blamer as if he or she is being dismissed and invalidated; that person then doesn't feel heard.

This is why it is important to respond to blaming messages by separating the content of the message from the blame, as discussed in Chapter 6. In other words, just because someone screws up doesn't make him or her a screw-up.

Justifying: Most of the time, justifying happens when someone doesn't meet his or her goals. In relationships, especially in arguments, people will often justify their own behavior as a way of not taking responsibility for what they have done. People generally use justification to deflect responsibility for their actions in two big ways. The first way is by claiming that another person's behavior *caused* the first person's actions. When one person points out something another did wrong, it's typical for the first person to respond, "I did *that* because you did *this*."

My friend Aaron shared a good example of this with me. When he woke up late one Saturday morning, he hurried to get ready for work. He emptied an ice cube tray, threw a few ice cubes in his coffee, and didn't bother to refill the tray before leaving for the office. When he got home, his wife Cammi said, "You left the ice cube tray out on the stove this morning," in a tone Aaron described as halfway between matter-of-fact and disapproving.

"I was running late because you kept me up so late talking with your friends at your dinner party last night," he responded. Aaron was implying that *Cammi* was responsible for Aaron's not re-filling the ice cube tray because their dinner party (which he referred to as "her" dinner party) caused him to be up late, which in turn contributed to him to getting up late and being in a hurry to get to work. Cammi didn't feel heard or appreciated. This simple exchange escalated into a fight about Aaron not appreciating all the things his wife does around the house.

"If I were a smart man, which I am not," Aaron said when he told me about the argument, "I would have said, 'Yes, honey, I did leave the tray out. I am sorry. I was in a hurry and I didn't mean to make more work for you. I don't thank you enough for everything you do. Thank you for re-filling the tray for me.'"

Another way some people use justifying to avoid taking responsibility for their behavior is to claim that because they're correct about the facts of an argument, the other person has no grounds to feel the way they feel, dismissing that person's feelings. This particular dynamic is such a big issue that I've devoted an entire chapter to it (Chapter 16).

When we do not take responsibility for our actions and feelings, we are attempting to dismiss the importance of the consequences we have created in our lives or to ignore that such consequences exist. In doing this, we sidestep our power to make the necessary changes that can make our lives better and our dreams come true.

Accepting responsibility for our lives and feeling our own power is an intense experience. We were given the power to create the lives of which we have dreamed. This is where the first pillar (It's Not About Joy or Pain, but Intensity) comes into play; we have to be able to handle the intensity of our own feelings to be able to step into our own power. So often the adaptations we make to deaden the intensity of our painful experiences when combined with low self-worth cut us off from feeling our own power and knowing we have a right to step into our power in any relationship.

How Do Arguments Happen?

Arguments can destroy the heart of a relationship. Most couples have no idea how they start their conflicts with each other. When they learn how their arguments happen, they can also learn to identify all the points along the way where each of them have made choices and have responded to their feelings in ways that have escalated fights. The skills and awareness needed to end arguments can also keep arguments from happening in the first place.

When I ask clients, "What do each of you have to do to create an argument?" the initial story I get paints one picture. But when I get the whole story, the picture looks quite different. The story usually starts off like this: "He was in a bad mood and that got *me* in a bad mood. Then he started yelling at me for no reason and we argued for an hour."

When I asked a patient named Clare to tell me about what went wrong in her relationship with her boyfriend, she told me, "He broke up with me when I asked him for support while my mom was in the hospital." After quite a bit of digging, the rest of the story came out. She eventually shared, "I don't blame him for leaving. I have been scared since we got together. Instead of facing my fear, I have spent the last two years being bossy and controlling. I try to control every aspect of his life. It's like I choke the life out of him and then try to force him to have sex with me to try to prove to myself that we are okay. Of course he wants to leave me and doesn't want to have sex with me—I have been smothering him."

"What would you have to do to re-create this whole situation with your boyfriend?" I asked her.

"Why would I want to do that?" Clare responded. "I don't ever want to go through this ever again."

"I don't want you too either," I assured her. "You need to know exactly how to re-create it so you will have a sense of what *not* to do anymore. Otherwise, you will do it again."

"It's so f#@ked up," she said.

"Then let's write out a perfect prescription for how to create a totally f#@ked up relationship," I suggested, starting to take notes.

"Well, I would have to start with avoiding the grief from my previous marriage," Clare began. "I am not okay being alone, so I asked him to stay with me initially so I didn't have to face my fear of being alone." She discussed how her fear of being alone was compounded by being scared of her boyfriend hanging out with his friends, most of whom she didn't like because they had criminal lifestyles. "So I would also have to ignore the fact that I don't want to date someone who prefers to hang out with criminals and try to control him so I don't ever have to face the fact that he may not be the kind of guy I really want in the first place."

"Is there anything you can do when problems come up?" I asked. "How would you have to respond to him to make it even more f#@ked up?"

She thought about it for a while, and over the next 15 minutes, Clare put together the following list: "First, act like the pitiful anxious girl: 'Please don't go hang out with Greg! I can't take it, honey. I am begging you! I don't want to think about what could happen.' Then, if he protests, immediately turn into the angry girl: 'You Mother F#@ker! You have no right to treat me this way!' Then, act like the catastrophe girl: 'This is horrible. Why does everything go wrong in my life? I can't ever seem to do the right thing. This is all my fault!'" Admitting that she hated being this manipulative, Clare added, "You would be surprised how effective it is."

"I bet," I responded. "You can get him to do pretty much what you want. The problem is that he is loath to be around you; he is cut-off from his desire, and now he is gone."

"Yeah," she said. "I guess it isn't the best way to go about it."

"But you are leaving out the best part," I continued. "You have to do the opposite of what you are doing right here with me."

"You mean telling the truth?" she asked.

"When you came in, you started with, 'I asked for support and he left me,'" I explained. "If you go to him and say, 'I asked you for support while my mother was in the hospital and you frickin' left me,' it sounds like an accusation, and it sounds like you did nothing to precipitate him feeling fed up. He is not going to respond very well to that because his reserves are just about empty on a daily basis anyway, and you pestered him even more, squeezed him even tighter, while your mom was in the hospital."

"Yeah, I do that all the time," Clare said, shaking her head. "I never take responsibility for my part. I act like he's the one who does everything wrong and I get off scot free." Then, with a confused expression, she sarcastically asked, "Is that the kind of thing that is worthy of an apology?"

"Yeah, maybe," I said with a sarcastic laugh. "Just maybe."

Again, the truth is that we co-create our relationships. When we don't take responsibility for our part in co-creating the messes, the stories we often tell about the messes come out sounding like we are victims. Our partners often feel like we are accusing them of creating all the problems we face. We have all been wrongfully accused of doing something in our lives that we didn't do. It can be infuriating, unless we have the confidence and assuredness in ourselves to accept the other person's accusation and know that we have not done anything wrong. When we are confident in our own worth, we can hear another's accusation and recognize it for what it is: hurt feelings.

It's Not Fair!

Life is not fair. Relationships are not fair. It is not fair that someone else has opportunities that you do not have. It is not fair that some people seem to achieve success without much effort. It is not fair for someone to wrongfully accusing you of being solely responsible for the problems in an intimate relationship because that person is too scared to take responsibility for his or her part of what is happening. You are right, it's not fair. *So what?*

Whining about something not being fair does not make the situation better. Complaining about fairness does not make things fair or put things back into balance. Whining and complaining that life is not fair is the same as telling God you want to stay stuck and feel powerless. This sets you up for sadness and reinforces a victim mindset because it keeps you from coming up with empowered solutions.

When we tell a story of being powerless, we are thinking powerlessly and we feel powerless. Creating a new habit of thinking powerfully, accepting responsibility, and never blaming takes quite a bit of effort— just like establishing any new habit. *This habit is worth it!*

Our job in this lifetime is to love. When we are complaining, feeling sorry for ourselves, blaming, or feeling less than worthy, *we are not loving!* Accepting life "as is" is a *huge* element of loving ourselves, loving each other, and building a great life. Without this acceptance, it is hard to gain clarity about the initial steps we need to take to effect meaningful, powerful change.

When life gives you unfair situations, remember that the events that made the unfairness are immediately in the past and unable to be changed. Complaining does not change the past, so it cannot change the unfair situation you are complaining about. Complaining does not motivate you or anyone to make empowered changes.

Jean learned this when she came into the office with pretty serious anxiety. She talked about her four-year-old autistic grandson and how his autism had been a challenge for her. She could hardly spend time with him when he was younger because she would get so sad being around him. She shared that she was so mad at God for making this little boy autistic. Eventually, she got to a point where she loved spending a lot more time with her grandson, even though she still struggled with thinking, *It's not fair.*

Saying, "It's not fair" insinuates that the circumstances of our lives need to be different for us to be happy. While some circumstances cannot be changed, what we *can* change is our response to the circumstances.

By feeling her love and doing a loving visualization similar to the ones outlined in Chapter 4, Jean was able to transform her emotional state and feel peaceful love instead of her usual soul-crushing angst whenever she thought of her grandson. Loving through unfortunate circumstances is the most empowering response we can have to the challenges life throws at us.

Few of us were taught growing up how to stand in our power. Often when the circumstances in our lives are not going the way we want, what we need is to feel our own personal power and presence. This necessitates having a sense of our genuine worth and rejecting fatalistic "things can never change" thinking.

PRACTICES:

- Become aware of when you complain, blame, and justify. Eliminate these behaviors from your life. When you complain, blame, and justify, you are declaring to the world that you cannot ever get what you want. Instead, say what you want, stating it simply and firmly.
- When you feel you are being treated unfairly, ask yourself the following questions: *How have I contributed to this situation? What can I change about the situation? What can I not change about the*

situation? Can I get help, and if so, from whom? Can I grow big enough to overcome this problem?

- When you are in an argument, ask yourself what you are willing to share with the other person and what you are *not* willing to share. Then ask yourself what would happen if you shared what it is that you are afraid to share.

Chapter 11

Listening

One of the biggest triggers for couples fighting is not feeling heard or not feeling that your partner understands or even acknowledges your pain. In order to become collaborative partners in solving any problems you face in your relationship, you must practice the skill of listening. The most common obstacle that gets in the way of this is trying to win.

If you and I are arguing and my goal is to win the argument, I will need to disprove what you say. If I can prove that what you are saying is wrong, then I must be right (at least according to the way most people argue). While this is a great plan if you are a defense attorney who wants to establish reasonable doubt in a court case, it's not such a useful plan for couples building a relationship. In fact, it's a horrible plan that can have devastating long-term consequences.

Intimacy is not adversarial. As the saying goes, you can either be right or you can be happy (more about this in Chapter 16). When you and your partner argue to win, you both lose. If you are listening only for your next chance to prove your partner wrong, your partner isn't going to feel heard, understood, or cared for. That's no way to maintain closeness and build trust. While you and your partner may enjoy witty banter and arguing as a manner of flirting and excitement, the heart of intimacy is *vulnerability*.

If I could teach only one lesson about listening, it would be this: Listen as if what your partner is upset about has nothing to do with you!

Most of the time when people are upset with you, it really *isn't* about you. Usually you have just triggered one of their issues. Even if it *is* about you, you need to hear what the other person has to say. If he or she is being abusive, then you need to set boundaries. If the other person is not being abusive, you need to listen—without judging yourself *or* the other person. Try to learn more about how your partner feels and encourage him or her to share more by saying things like, "Tell me more," "What else?" "I am still listening, I'd like to hear more."

I advise couples to listen to their partners in an argument as if they are trying to gather all the information necessary to be able to make their partners' arguments for them. For example, when my wife and I are talking, I want to listen so intently that I understand how she is feeling, why she is feeling that way, and what she wants. I want to understand what is going on with her so well that I can repeat back to her exactly how she feels in my own words—so much so that if we switched places, I could argue her point just as well as she could. In doing that, I better understand her and know her in those moments, and she has a better chance of believing that I truly hear what she's saying.

When your partner feels heard, he or she is much less reactive and much more likely to listen to you in return—and that helps build a foundation for trust. How your partner feels needs to be just as important to you as how you feel. If you ignore your own feelings in order to try to make your partner happy, or if you ignore your partner's feelings to try to make yourself happy, you're avoiding authenticity. Instead, I want you and your partner to both feel heard and honored.

Listening with a Compassionate Heart

Ask your partner if he or she is willing to do a listening practice with you. If your partner agrees, have your partner lie down on his or her back and get comfortable. Lie beside your partner on your side, facing him or her. Put your hand on your partner's stomach or on your partner's heart. Say, "I am listening. I would like to hear anything you would like to share." As your partner shares, make the commitment to listen for as long as your partner needs or wants to talk. Listen in order to understand your partner's perspective on whatever he or she is talking about. If your partner takes a long pause, just breathe and wait. If your partner begins getting angry and starts making defensive statements, very gently remind your partner to share his or her feelings by saying something like, "What does that feel like?"

As you listen, notice the difference between what your partner is sharing and your own thoughts and perspective (those thoughts that are important to *you*, and those points that *you* may want your partner to consider) and then *let those thoughts go!* This is your time to be receptive and to take your partner in. Notice when you want to interrupt to point something out that you think is important. Especially take notice of when you are judging that your partner is wrong. All of the things you want to interject as well as all of your judgments become *your* agenda for the other person. When you notice your own agenda, take a breath and let it go because those thoughts are getting in the way of you being able to hear your partner. Rest assured that you will have your time to share later. This is a time for you to listen. Even if you are a really good listener already, use this exercise to develop this skill even more.

If your partner seems to stop and you sense that he or she still has more to share, simply say, "I am still listening." It is rare in our society for people to get the chance to express themselves fully. It can be healing to keep the door open for someone else to share more and say all of what he or she has to say. Try this practice with the intent of honoring how your partner feels, what your partner thinks, and how he or she sees the world. If you want to be close to your partner, you have to get close to how he or she is feeling. This includes *accepting* how your partner feels. He or she will see things differently than you do, and getting closer requires that you understand and honor both the other's perspective and the other's right to feel that way. When your partner is truly finished and has nothing else to share, thank him or her for sharing.

This practice, as with any solid listening practice, is not only an integral step in making sure your partner feels heard, but it can also be an excellent meditative practice for you to notice those judgments and thoughts that keep you from being fully present with your partner.

FAIR FIGHTING

When you and your partner are having a heated argument, the Listening with a Compassionate Heart practice is probably not one you'll be willing to try—although it would be awesome if you did! Couples embroiled in conflict often need a more structured method. I suggest the Fair Fighting process (a conflict resolution technique that became popular in the 1980s). The skills embedded in the Fair Fighting process can transform the way you and your partner listen and share with each other. It not only provides a constructive format for dealing with disagreement, but it also can de-escalate an argument and help you end ongoing conflicts.

While I believe that any couple could benefit from using this process, it may feel too restrictive to some. In that case, if you have already developed some degree of mindfulness about your own process and emotions, the Listening with a Compassionate Heart practice may be a better fit and the only practice you need to enrich your connection when dealing with tense topics. But those who are simply resistant to trying anything that would make them vulnerable are the ones who could benefit the most from Fair Fighting because it will give them the experience of feeling heard and finding resolution to a conflict without having a heated battle.

I know Fair Fighting works because I've studied the results myself. When I was an undergraduate at the University of Tennessee in Knoxville, I was part of a research team headed by my father, the late Marcus L. Ambrester, Jr., Ph.D., a professor of Communications. In conducting a study that contributed to one of my father's books, *Communicating through Conflict: An Interpersonal Perspective*, the team gathered stories from couples about their conflict patterns. Several of the couples interviewed who had already gone through my father's Communicating Through Conflict training program had made the commitment to use Fair Fighting on a regular basis. These couples reported that their conflicts were no longer destructive to their relationships. Using the skills they learned in Fair Fighting, they had transformed their fights into opportunities to get closer and to build authentic intimacy.

The process starts with the following ground rules:

1. Both people have to agree to Fair Fight.
2. No hitting below the belt. This means not intentionally saying things that you know will hurt the other person's feelings. For example, instead of saying, "Then you did that thing, just like your mother, where you swallowed all your anger," instead say, "Then I expected you to get mad and you got quiet."
3. No wearing your belt around your head. This means it's not okay to act as if *everything* the other person says is a hit below the belt. (In short, *no drama!*)

Before you begin, agree who will go first or flip a coin. (I once had a couple call me because they were fighting about who was going to go first!) For simplicity, instead of saying "Person A" and "Person B," I will use "he" and "she." (I actually flipped a coin when writing this to see who would go first in my description.)

Step 1: He shares his recollection of the events that happened around the subject of the fight. He shares just the facts, listing only the physical events that happened. It is important that he describe the events with no characterizations and without assigning motives. This is not the time to include why he did something or why he thinks that she did something. It would be a violation of the Fair Fighting protocols to say, "Then you said, '_____' just to hurt me," because adding the phrase "just to hurt me" is assigning motives. This time is for him to state only his recollection of the events.

Step 2: She repeats *his* account of the events from *his* perspective, and to his satisfaction. Whether or not she *agrees* with what he gives as the order of events, she restates his account of the events. When she is finished re-telling his account of the events, she asks him if she left anything out. He reminds her of anything that she did not include, and she then re-states his account and includes it, demonstrating that she is hearing his story.

Step 3: She shares her recollection of the events that happened around the subject of the fight. This is not the time for her to try to prove his account of the events wrong. This is a chance for her to tell her part of the story. Again, she should share just the facts. This is not the time for feelings, characterizations, or motives.

Step 4: He repeats *her* account of the events from *her* perspective, and to her satisfaction. When he has finished re-stating her account of the facts, he asks if she is satisfied with his telling of what she remembers. She reminds him of anything that he missed, just as he did for her above.

Step 5: He shares his feelings that came up during the incident as well as his current feelings. "When _____ happened, I felt _____. Then, when _____ happened, I felt _____."

Step 6: She paraphrases *his* feelings to his satisfaction.

Step 7: She shares her feelings that came up during the incident as well as her current feelings, following the same "When _____ happened, I felt _____" format. When he shared his feelings in Step 5 and she paraphrased them in Step 6, she may have gotten triggered. It is important to remember here in Step 7 that there's a difference between her stating her feelings and using the time to talk, arguing against the things that he said he was feeling. If she is sharing her feelings without any attachment to changing his mind, then he's going to perceive her as more authentic and will have less combative feelings in the interaction. The authenticity fosters more closeness.

Step 8: He paraphrases *her* feelings to her satisfaction.

Step 9: He offers a potential resolution.

Step 10: She restates his proposed resolution to his satisfaction and responds to his proposal, either accepting it or, if necessary, offering a counter-proposal to include both her concerns and his concerns.

Step 11: If she offered a counter-proposal, he then restates her counter-proposal to her satisfaction and responds. They continue this pattern until they both agree on a proposal for potential resolution of the conflict.

Most of the time, when one person begins genuinely listening, the other begins to feel more comfortable acknowledging his or her feelings and then sharing those feelings. Usually by Step 6 or Step 8, both people are listening really well and are no longer trying to win the fight; instead, they are cooperating and collaborating. And that's the key. For Fair Fighting to work, both people have to be willing to get in touch with and share what they are feeling.

If I am not willing to feel my feelings, or if I want to pretend I am not feeling anything, then there is no way that I can talk about my feelings. Yet when I share what I'm feeling without any attachment to the other person agreeing with me, I'm sharing from a more authentic place. Authenticity is what creates closeness—*not* agreeing with each other. We can have two very different perspectives and still feel close to and supported by each other.

The real magic of Fair Fighting is that each person learns to hold the other's feelings and thoughts in equal importance to his or her own. When people quit listening for the chance to discredit the other and they start sharing openly and honestly, then they don't need the Fair Fighting format anymore.

Some couples are so embroiled in conflict that they need lots of practice. (As a client of mine named Meg once shared with her partner, "I know we disagree. I need you to understand how I am feeling and I need you to know it is okay for me to feel this way, even though you feel differently." Pausing briefly, Meg then added, "Sweetie, if you can't do that, I am going to have to kill you.") Sometimes I will have such couples practice Fair Fighting in my office. When one of them gets triggered, reacts, and starts arguing, I have them stop the Fair Fight and focus on resolving whatever got triggered. Once that person calms down, he or she is then able to share what's going on inside in an appropriate way. Then, the couple can pick the Fair Fight back up where they left off.

Conflict doesn't have to suck and it doesn't have to tear relationships apart. Conflict is destructive only when a couple does not have the emotional, listening, and communication skills necessary to handle disagreements well.

PRACTICES:

- Practice listening with your partner by arguing each other's positions about a subject where you disagree. Begin by listening to how your partner feels, and then switch places and make your partner's point yourself. Then have your partner listen to how you feel and have him or her argue your point for you.
- At a time when you and your partner are not in the heat of an argument, try talking at the same time. Whenever either one of you doesn't feel heard (which should happen pretty quickly, since it is impossible to talk and listen at the same time), talk louder. This exercise can get *really* loud, *really* fast, and it often ends with both people laughing hysterically and recognizing that the exercise resembles how they argue when they *are* actually upset with each other.
- Whenever your partner is talking, take a breath and feel how you feel listening to the other person. After he or she is finished, say, "As you were talking, I was feeling _____."
- In any discussion you choose, wait five seconds before responding. During this time, take a breath. The person may have more to say, or you may find that the five seconds gives you a chance to take in what was said on a deeper level.
- Make a commitment to knowing your partner as well as you can. If you don't understand how he or she feels about something or if you don't understand how he or she could feel that way, say, "I want to understand what you are saying and I am not quite getting it, so please keep going."
- When you want to talk about something important, turn off the television, turn off your cell phone ringer, lock the kids in a closet, give the dog a treat, and set aside the time and space to be able to talk without distractions. Begin by saying, "You are important to me. I want to be able to give you my full attention, without any distractions."

CHAPTER 12

INTEGRITY

Integrity has two definitions. The first, adherence to moral and ethical principles, involves telling the truth—doing what you say you are going to do, and *not* doing what you say you are *not* going to do. The second definition, the state of being whole or undiminished, is the one I want to focus on here. That is about your responsibility to bring *all* of who you are into the world. We each have unique gifts and experiences, and sharing those gifts in their entirety is the reason we're here.

As my spiritual teacher once told me, the world doesn't need any more people playing it safe, just going through the motions. Playing small is not a virtue, because then the world misses out on the piece you were meant to bring. This is not to say that everyone has to be in the spotlight or that working a 9-5 job to support a family instead of becoming rich and famous is in any way inadequate. What it means is that it is not okay to walk a path that is not your own true path; you were meant to walk a path where you are doing what you love!

The excitement, creativity, and vision that are within us are among the most powerful resources we could ever have. Our thoughts, our brainpower, our problem-solving skills, and our ability to plan are all incredibly valuable tools—yet they are completely and utterly *useless* if we are not in touch with who we truly are and with what God put us here to do in the first place.

You were meant to walk a certain path in life that is *your* path to walk—the path of your highest self. It is the path that excites you, the path of your dreams, although it probably also scares you and may even seem impossible (at least at first). Walking this path requires you to walk in balance, fully integrating your spiritual life, your emotions, your physical health, and your thoughts so that *all* of who you are is available at every moment. Walking your true path is the only way to play big, no matter what that looks like (and it will look *different* for every person).

REMEMBER TO BREATHE

If you don't know what you are here for, it's time to get clear. Start with the breathing exercises outlined in Chapter 9, making time to breathe on a daily basis. Breathing is essential because it helps you get in touch with the pain you need to heal so that you can clearly see your gifts. Without breathing, you will not feel your own energy emerging, and you won't feel your own excitement—you probably won't even be able to tell the difference between genuine feelings in your heart and thoughts that are in your head. As a seven-year-old friend of mine, a very wise "pint-sized shaman," once told her mother, "Spirit speaks to us through our hearts. What you hear in your head is just your fear."

It's time to begin clearing out the crap about who you think you should be, who you were told you ought to be, and who you think you need to be. You may even feel like a client of mine who once told me, "But I don't *have* a self. I am just a to-do list."

I have asked a few clients who feel this way to pull out their to-do lists. Of course, they have their lists with them, and they get them right out and show them to me. They're very proud. Their lists are very organized and very neat. I take the piece of paper they show me and I crumble it up and ask, "Now, who are you?" Sometimes this elicits panic, but most of the time, people have a moment where they just take a breath. I ask again in a calmer, more affirming tone, "Who are you? Just feel what it feels like to be you—right this second, sitting right there."

So I will ask you the same question. Right now, as you are reading this book, take a breath and then take a moment to feel what it feels like to be you right this second. Make your only concern at this moment feeling your own energy.

When we do not *embrace* and *express* all of who we are, we have the experience of something being missing or not fully being met in relationships. Being fully present is our natural state. We don't have to ask newborns to feel their feelings; we don't ever sense that infants are hiding their true selves. Yet as we grow into adolescence, we learn social norms and how to fit in. We are all hardwired for social connection, and only when we are hurting do we deny the importance of having other people in our lives. However, that drive for social connection can also get in the way of authentic growth if our social influences are not healthy ones.

What Gets in the Way

We learn thousands of ways to not bring all of who we are to our relationships. The most common dynamic that keeps us from doing this is the fear of being unacceptable in another's eyes. Many of us feel an enormous social pressure to fit in, to be accepted. Due to society's deficiency in honoring each person's own unique value, we struggle to know we are okay. In an effort to fit in and gain approval, we all learn to *not* show the world all of who we are. If we sense that what we are feeling is not acceptable to others (whether those others are important to us or not), it can feel like *we* are not acceptable. This is why it is so important to separate *worth* and *behavior* (as we talked about in Chapter 6), or in this case, *worth* and *feeling*. If we sense disapproval or non-acceptance, we must either face the possibility of not being accepted (which can trigger a fear of rejection if we have the kind of attachment issues we discussed in Chapter 5) or we must change how much of our true selves we share with others.

When we hide who we are on a regular basis, telling ourselves we're justified in doing so because we need to be accepted, it can become a way of life. One of the biggest hindrances to personal growth is not finding a circle of our true peers who value us in our individuality. As we meet our attachment and worthiness needs, however, we will have the courage to step out of societal norms and to put others' expectations aside so we can discover what's the right fit for us.

I assure you, people who will welcome all of who you are *do exist* in the world! All you have to do is have the courage to ask for them to come into your life, and then be willing to say "yes" when you meet them. This often involves a slow transition to a new way of being with new friends and new circles of acquaintances. The more you embrace all of who you are, the more people you will meet who will also embrace all of you, and the more acceptance you will get from the people who are already in your life now.

Every Feeling Is Either Showing Us Who We Are or What Needs to Heal

Once we get over the hurdle of fearing that we may not be acceptable, the next task is to be clear about who we really are. How do you know who you are so that you will be able to bring all of who you are to the world? Great question! It's also a trick question because it is impossible to answer in normal reality. You simply can't know the immensity of Who You Are. It's like trying to hold running water in your hand. It's fluid, ever changing, and always evolving.

For example, if I am feeling down, does that mean that I am a depressed person? In that moment, yes it does. In the next moment, if I am happy, does that mean I am a happy person? Yes it does. The labels "depressed person" or "happy person" are mere evaluations, and they're mostly useless. They are cognitive constructs about our genuine being-ness. The labels we place on our experience are not the same as the experience itself. The experience itself holds gifts. Our evaluation of our experience may help to diagnose problems, but it cannot encapsulate the vastness of who we are as people. So when someone says to me, "I am depressed," I don't really care about that person's assessment because the explanation for why a person thinks he or she is depressed keeps the person stuck in his or her head. Instead, I want to hear what the person is doing that leads to this assessment of feeling depressed.

So to discover who you really are, don't search for labels. And don't cast your net too wide. Start thinking in terms of who you are *right now—right this second.* The most readily available information you have about who you are is what you are feeling at this moment. We all have feelings all the time. Bringing your awareness to your feelings in the present moment will allow you to enjoy the enjoyable moments, heal the hurt feelings that are keeping you from living the life you want, and clear the way to take actions that are congruent with meeting your goals. This will help bridge the gap between who you are and who you want to be. In essence, all the information you need to make your life what you want it to be is available right now, encoded in your feelings.

When doing this work, it's important not to judge your feelings or judge yourself for having them. If you don't like a particular feeling, that means you most definitely need to feel it! That feeling is trying to tell you something about yourself that you need to know. When you judge it, you're pushing it away and so you're no longer present. Fully feeling your feelings is the only way to experience who you are in this moment.

Your next step, only after having the experience of feeling your feelings, is to evaluate if the way you feel is consistent with who you want to be. If your feelings aren't in line with your goals, it is time to dig to the roots of those feelings. You may discover that your feelings are coming from a hurt that needs to heal. (Any time you're not feeling love, joy, and gratitude, it is a sign that some kind of hurt is affecting your awareness and trying to be expressed.) Or maybe your heart is leading you in a different direction that your so-called logical thinking had rejected or not considered. I hear people say, "Don't listen to your feelings. You can't trust them." It's the people saying such things who I don't trust. If you go only by what's in your head and you don't pay attention to what's in your heart, then you can end up doing things that don't really fit who you are. And where is the genuineness in that?

Who Will You Be in the Future?

You can't know who you will be in the future because you haven't become that person yet. You may *never* become who you *think* you might be, so recognize those thoughts as mere fantasies. Then use those fantasies to set goals, and accept that you determine your future by the choices you make and the actions you take *right now*. Keep in mind that as the future gets here, your fantasy of how things were going to look may be very different from the plan that God has for you.

Who You Were in the Past

Trying to figure out who we were in the past is pointless. Everything we need to know about our past is a part of us and will come out when it needs to in how we are feeling right at that moment. Our past is a story, plain and simple. We cannot change the events of the past, but we can change how we tell the story. It is important to have a good story to tell, and the story must be authentic if we are to have an awesome life. If the story we tell is not exciting and inspiring, full of love and gratitude, then we need to make peace with some pieces of our history.

Maybe you have never accepted the death of a loved one or never fully healed from a trauma of rape, violence, or molestation. Whatever happened, you cannot change it, but you *can* heal the hurt. Often, that requires forgiveness. *True* forgiveness is when you have healed so thoroughly from an offense that you do not feel as if any wrong was done to you. (As Mark Twain once said, "Forgiveness is the fragrance that the violet sheds on the heel that has crushed it.") If you have truly forgiven, when you think of the incident, you are thankful for the experience because you needed the lessons and the gifts that you received in the healing. As horrible as some of those experiences may have been, they do bring gifts into your life. We certainly prefer gentle and clear lessons, but the truth is that we don't get to make that choice. The choice we *do* get to make is to either paint ourselves as victims or to heal.

Your capacity for forgiveness is your capacity "for-giving" love. Only when you have healed the hurt of an offense are you are able to feel and give love again. If you are not feeling love and gratitude, then you haven't fully forgiven. Even if you generally love someone, you can still hold a grudge or resentment. In one moment you are feeling and giving your love and in the next moment you are not giving love because you are thinking of your grudge and the offense. The expression, "I forgive, but I don't forget," is not an expression of forgiveness. Of course we may never forget being hurt, although the incident will not carry the same emotional charge when the hurt is healed.

Often when someone gets hurt, the lesson is about boundaries that weren't set or weren't honored. When the person was hurt as a child, he or she wasn't capable of setting an appropriate boundary at that time. Always maintaining safe boundaries is important. When someone says, "I don't forget," he or she is talking about maintaining healthy boundaries. Forgiveness means not holding a past hurt against another, and it does *not* mean being open to being hurt again or going back to a way of being that puts a person at risk for being hurt again.

My Other Car Is a Ferrari

Imagine that you are stopped at a red light and a 30-year-old car is in front of you. This car is covered in rust, has a broken windshield, and displays a bumper sticker that says, "My other car is a Ferrari." Do you think the person driving that car *really* owns a Ferrari?

Now, if you love Ferraris and you want to marry a man who has one, you might marry this guy based on the promise he states on his bumper sticker. When you get to his run-down, one-bedroom apartment, you don't see a Ferrari parked outside. Of course, he tells you the car is in the shop. After a couple of years, you noticed that his Ferrari still hasn't been fixed and you still haven't gotten to ride in it. Chances are you would eventually end up in my office complaining that your husband lied to you, that he is such an idiot, and that you are having a hard time trusting him and forgiving him. Who is the real idiot here? While this example is a great exaggeration, it's the same basic story I hear over and over.

Here's a real-life example. Janie came in complaining that her boyfriend Josh was having an online affair. "He said he was sorry, so I forgave him," she told me. "Then he did it again. This has been happening the whole time we have been together." Janie expected that because Josh apologized, he wouldn't hurt her again, even though he exhibited the same behaviors leading up to the hurt as he had always done. She had a gut feeling that something was not right, but she ignored her inner voice. She chose to act as if he was telling the truth about stopping his internet trysts, and then she acted as if she couldn't believe that he had been having more of them. Janie *had* been wronged, but not just by Josh (as she contended). Janie had wronged *herself* by not honoring her own feelings. She ignored her own sense that Josh was lying to her.

"Just because someone tells you that he is telling the truth, it doesn't mean he is *not* lying to you," I told Janie. "Even if he tells you that he is telling the truth, you still have to decide for yourself if you believe him. You chose to act as if you believed him, even though you obviously did not."

Janie soon broke up with Josh and held her grudge against him for a long time. Only after she took responsibility for her own choice to ignore her inner sense did she quit feeling resentment toward her former boyfriend. Then, when a guy she had started to date began exhibiting the same patterns, Janie noticed when she started to ignore her inner voice, which told her the guy was lying to her.

"Thank God for Josh," she told me the next time she came in. "I am *not* making that mistake again! I guess since I thanked God for Josh, I must really have forgiven him," she added with pride. "I am actually thankful to have learned that lesson in such a big way."

"So you're not mad at Josh for being an idiot anymore?" I asked.

"Well," she said with a smile. "He's still an idiot. But I don't blame him for it."

Forgiving Ourselves

As Janie did, sometimes when we look back, we can clearly see that we could have prevented some of the hurts or wrongs we experienced. But beating ourselves up for not doing then what we would do in the same situation now is a horrible waste of time. Only in having the experience can we learn the valuable lessons necessary *not* to do what we did the first time. In order to forgive ourselves for something we wish we hadn't done, or for *not* doing something we wish we *had* done, we must give ourselves permission to learn from our mistakes. We must accept the fact that we didn't realize the magnitude of the situation at the time and that we have learned or are learning not to make the same mistakes again. The experience of hurting and healing can be a brutal teacher, and we sometimes need those lessons in just that way in order to get it. Having a great life is not about not having big problems. It's about how we respond to our challenges, both big and small.

QUIT TRYING TO DO IT "RIGHT"

I recently saw a client who lives with the constant fear of not pleasing her boss, not pleasing her husband, and not pleasing her mother ("who can never be pleased"). She said that when she was in school, she actually felt calm because she had a very clear set of instructions about what she needed to do to please her instructors and get good grades. After she graduated and got married, she lived in a constant frantic state of "trying to do it right."

"Once I was out in the world," she told me, "I felt as though the world demanded so much of me that I couldn't take it anymore."

We all grow up with a sense of what it means to do it "right." We get that sense of right and wrong from the "Am I okay?" stage of development that we discussed in Chapter 6. As toddlers, part of our motivation is to make our parents happy. If we don't have a healthy balance between knowing our own worth and gaining others' approval, we become anxious about doing things "right," have little tolerance for disappointing others, or feel the need to gain approval from anyone who may remotely resemble an authority figure. Part of maturing emotionally calls for developing our own standards by which we want to live. We set ourselves up for a life of misery when we base our worth on making someone else (including an internalized "someone," such as the voice of a disapproving parent) happy.

A more worthy goal is to make ourselves happy by accepting who we are and by becoming all of who we want to be in the world. Sometimes we have to accept ourselves before we can begin to live up to our own standards, and sometimes setting and striving for our own standards is what helps us begin to accept ourselves. Either way, by getting in touch with all of our feelings, we can begin to get in touch with our gifts. And by using those gifts, we are, in essence, making God very happy.

Psychotherapist Alyson Schwabe once said to me, "Spirit is not a disapproving parent. You don't have to do things right for Spirit to love you." God doesn't want us to be afraid of doing it "wrong." If fact, God knows that it is not possible to love in the presence of fear. Fear-based thinking is not a sign of genuine communion with God. The only true sin is to not be true to who you are.

Trying to please someone else is never as empowering as being the best that we can be by embracing and using our God-gifted talents for ourselves, for our families, and as a way of giving thanks to God. Although some of the ideas we were taught when we were young about socially acceptable behavior ("Don't hit your sister!" "Don't run with scissors!") are truly good for us as well as for others, many aren't so black-and-white. As healthy adults, we must walk our own paths and quit trying to do the things we feel we "should" or "must" do. Social acceptability needn't get in the way of doing what is right and it needn't get in the way of being in service using God's gifts and doing God's work. So make sure you're not "shoulding" on yourself.

My wife knows all about this concept. She was always thinking she should be better and that she should be able to do everything without support. She'd tell herself that she should be able to take four college classes and still be a perfect mother, she should be able to support her husband and keep the house clean. The simple truth is that she *can't* do it all without being crazy.

One night, I praised her for going to bed and leaving dirty dishes in the sink. "Yep, I hung up my cape," she told me. "No more trying to be superwoman." I made sure I got up early and did the dishes before she got up to show her that she indeed did not have to do *everything* on her own. I am thankful she hung up her cape. Because I much prefer her not being crazy, I fully support her in not "shoulding" on herself.

These "shoulds" that we have when we're trying to live up to someone else's standards are different than the goals we set based on who we are and who we are meant to be in the world. Reaching realistic goals feels good. It is exciting to feel ourselves come more fully into our own lives, following a clarity of purpose and divine guidance.

Likewise, when you have a mentor, a life coach, or a therapist who pushes you very hard, trying to please that person can be a positive experience. The difference is that this is a person who will accept you no matter what you do, who will not take any credit for your successes, and who wants only the best for you. Such people are in your life in order to support you in achieving your own goals—not their goals for you according to their standards.

Although it feels good to have your efforts acknowledged, the bottom line is that the satisfaction you get in knowing that you've done a good job being who you are and who you want to be is greater than any praise you can get from someone else. When you can achieve this, you will no longer strive for security, love, trust, or worthiness. You will not struggle with perfectionism or self-doubt. By using your natural talents, you will love what you are doing, enjoy being who you are, and feel honored to bring your unique gifts to the planet—and everyone benefits.

PRACTICES:

- Make a list of the things you dream about and want in your life. In other words, if you could have everything you desire, how would you like your life to be? Then let yourself image having that life. *Feel* what that life would feel like to you. Notice if thoughts about how to make that life happen distract you. Instead, just stay with that feeling and watch out for the thought, *But that could never happen*.

- Think of three things that you have always felt you "should" be and that you are ready to admit don't really fit you anymore. Write them down and then make a statement that *does* fit you and speaks more to who you really are. Next, take these statements to someone you trust and say, "I have always believed that I should _____. Now, I am ready to embrace _____ about myself." Note that this is *not* about getting the other person's approval—it's about being genuine with someone *and* having someone else witness your being real.

- Think of something that is important to you that you have kept to yourself because you are afraid that someone would judge you if you shared it. Go to someone you trust and say, "I have always kept a secret because I was afraid of being judged, and now I am ready to share more of myself without shame." Then share your secret with the other person and pay attention to how good (and scary) it feels to be more fully seen by another.

CHAPTER 13

HOUSEWORK

I've always been amazed at how big an issue housework is in families and in marriages. One truth has become clear: It is never about the housework. Just like anything else, housework can only become an issue in a relationship if we respond poorly to our differences about household matters or to what gets triggered inside by household matters. Sometimes even more troublesome than talking about sexual issues, communication around housework seems to be one of the most polarizing and touchy subjects with which couples struggle. It is one of the subjects that almost always comes up when I'm working with a couple; and it is the area in which people seem to have both the least amount of introspective insight as well as the most resistance. In fact, some of my clients have navigated the horrible feelings around sexual abuse with more willingness than they give to considering changing their perspective on housework.

THE PLACE OF SPIRITUAL AND PHYSICAL REST

To understand why housework is such a trigger, we must first realize that most of us see our homes as sanctuaries where we ought to feel both physically and emotionally safe, secure, and at ease. For some people, what makes a home feel safe is what it *looks* like, while for others, it's how they *feel* when they're there. Often, problems come when one person in a couple needs to be responsibility-free to feel rested and restored, while his or her partner can't feel rested and restored until everything that has a place is in its place.

Housework can only become an issue for a couple if they are not addressing the *real* issues underlying their disagreement—most commonly issues of self-worth and safety/security/belonging. Self-worth issues often come out as judging oneself based on the appearance of the house, judging your partner about the way he or she keeps the house, and having either a desire to be appreciated or a feeling of not being appreciated. Belongingness issues can be more confusing because they can sometimes come out as a resistance to structure and rules, and at other times they surface as a need to control by setting a lot of rules. Although these two belongingness issues come from the same root, the variations look very different from each other.

We all get triggered sometimes. None of us is going to handle every situation perfectly when we get triggered, and that's okay. No matter how much healing work we have done, we get tossed back into early childhood patterns around something as seemingly benign as whether or not the dishes are done or the dirty socks are picked up. I have a tremendous respect for the couples who are willing to take responsibility for their own feelings and practice responsible communication when it comes to housework. When we get triggered about this issue or about anything else, we always have a choice. We can either blame our partner, which prevents us from *feeling* and *healing* the core hurt that is being triggered, *or* we can take responsibility for our triggered hurt, feel its intensity, and communicate our feelings in an appropriate way that fosters closeness and intimacy.

When someone gets triggered, he or she needs to address the triggered hurt directly. The discussion about the clutter, the dishes in the sink, or the socks left on the floor needs to be tabled until both people can discuss the matter without the extra weight of the triggered hurt clouding the discussion. Once couples address the triggered hurt, they often find that the housework issue is not an issue between them at all.

TOLERANCE LEVELS

Having different tolerance levels for cleanliness and clutter is just one of those funny, quirky things that makes us human and by itself, usually presents very little problem. If two people have different tolerance levels, it may seem that one person is ignoring clutter, while it may be the only thing the other person can see when he or she walks into a room. If you and your partner have different tolerance levels, you darn well better have the communication skills to make up for it! The other vital key is acceptance. Without that, it's easy to put the appearance of the house before the health of the communication between you. While you may find such acceptance frustrating, keep in mind these words attributed to Buddha: "Holding onto anger is like grasping a hot coal with the intent of throwing it at someone else; you are the one who gets burned."

Each story below shares an example of a different situation involving housework that couples have brought to me over the years. Each story is headed by a statement that a client made that triggered or escalated an argument. In each, I will point out some of the ways that poor communication can get us into trouble when it comes to talking with our beloved about cleaning the important safe havens that we call "home."

"I can't take all your rules. You are so *anal!*" This is what Gretchen screamed at her husband Bill one day. A gifted healer, Gretchen felt enormous responsibility at work and out in public to share her healing gifts with whoever needed them. When she got home, Gretchen wanted to be free from her responsibility to others and just take care of herself. In her mind, a safe haven and restorative space meant a place where no one put demands on her and where she could simply be herself without having to "be there" for anyone else. When Gretchen didn't get the emotional rest she needed, she felt run down, which triggered a deep wound around being worthless and not having a place in the world.

Bill, on the other hand, wanted the house to be very tidy, and he felt uneasy and agitated when things got messy. His work life felt so chaotic that coming home to a clean, neat house was his chance to relax emotionally. Gretchen's messiness made him feel as though he had to be on guard from the internal agitation he felt when he saw dresser drawers left open, lights left on, and plates on the coffee table. Underneath all his agitation was an underlying lack of self-worth. Bill's constant battle was to feel "good enough." At work, he was constantly being challenged and felt he had to prove himself and justify every decision he made. When he was at home, if the house was a mess, he heard his mother's voice in his head telling him, *Bill, you're a slob and you will never amount to anything.*

Housework became a constant struggle, triggering core issues for both Gretchen and Bill. For Gretchen, Bill's insistence to pick things up felt like personal rejection, triggering her sense of never belonging. Those issues came up in many aspects of their relationship, and their inability to heal the deeper issues ultimately led to their divorce. Their story illustrates how conflicts around housework can be an indicator of what needs to heal in a relationship.

"How can you just ignore all this stuff that *needs* to get done?" Dan thought his wife Carrie sounded judgmental when she asked him that question. He took the word "ignore" to imply that he was being irresponsible and felt that the word "need" was downright inflammatory—as though Carrie was insinuating that Dan was irresponsible if he did not do "all this stuff" immediately. The way he saw it, she *wanted* these things to be done and her *wanting* them done did not mean that they *needed* to be done. We all want to feel safe in our homes. If we feel judged or insulted, we don't feel safe.

Dan's mother had been a tyrant about housework and shamed her son as a way of motivating him to clean. As an adult, Dan rebelled against any show of authoritarianism in the home. The argument usually either turned into a debate about whether the cleaning really *needed* to be done or it turned into Dan saying, "If you want it cleaned, then clean it. You are the one who has a problem with it." The debate did not get to the heart of the matter and it did not bring them closer to each other. In this case, Dan was arguing against his own desire. Dan actually wanted the same household chores done that Carrie did. He was resisting doing them as a way of protesting against the perceived insinuation about his level of responsibility. When this couple brought this argument to me, we looked at various ways they could have avoided the fight.

Dan could have acknowledged his own triggers and responded with, "I just felt insulted and put down. I am not okay with the way the house looks either. If you want help, *ask me* for help." If he had said this, they both agreed, the fight could have been avoided because Dan would have been responding more genuinely to Carrie's statement.

Another possible solution they both liked was for Carrie to come to him and initially ask, "Sweetie, I am feeling a little tweaked about some household stuff that *I feel like* needs to get done. I want to do _____, _____, and _____, and I would like to get it all done in the next hour. Will you help me, please?"

"You mean I can just *ask* for what I want?" Carrie responded sarcastically. "That's a novel idea. But it's housework. Don't I have to be a bitch to get anything done?"

This couple usually did a great job of owning their own feelings until it came to housework. Even though Carrie had done quite a bit of healing work, she still felt herself get bossy and controlling when she thought the house was a mess. Dan was a pretty even-keeled guy who laughed at himself because when it came to housework, he said, "I still turn into that same rebellious little boy. At least I don't still take the trash bags out of my room and hide them under my mom's bed like I used to."

Our attitudes and beliefs around housework shed light on a depth of ourselves rarely reached outside the home. It is a scary thing to take on the task of looking into the issue of housework because most of our patterns and attitudes are set in childhood. Often, housework can seem like too silly of a topic to trigger such deep issues, so the deeper ramifications of these triggers are often dismissed.

"You go play all the time. You just leave everything and expect me to take care of it all." This sentiment and others like it usually come from different tolerance levels. Here's a personal story of how that can play out in relationships. In our house, my wife and I have two different dynamics around washing the dishes. The first dynamic is when there are three or four dirty dishes in the kitchen sink. The second is when the kitchen sink is over half-full of dishes.

If my wife puts a plate and two small bowls in an otherwise empty sink, my initial knee-jerk reaction is to think, *Is she just going to leave them there? It would be so easy to wash them now before they pile up*. Of course I don't say that; I recognize that it is my trigger and I will either wash the dishes or let it go. My wife, on the other hand, has infinite tolerance for three or four things in the sink. She can easily wait until there is a full load of dishes to do. Neither way is better, we simply have different preferences.

When the sink is over half-full, the tide turns. I can tolerate a mostly full sink of dishes about six hours longer than my wife can. On these occasions, my wife thinks, *He doesn't care, he just expects me to do it*. I don't pretend to understand how these tolerance levels get established. What makes the difference in our relationship is in how we each respond to the feelings we have around dishes in the sink.

After I had finished doing the dishes one night, my wife threw a couple of small bowls, two spoons, and a knife in the sink. "Oh sure, just run off and play!" I jokingly said to her. "You expect me to take care of it when you just throw things in the sink, don't you?" She didn't laugh. I tried it again several years later after we had both grown a lot. It was funnier the second time—and the third. She didn't even punch me!

"You only think about yourself. You don't ever consider my feelings." When Sara said this to her husband Tom, she was feeling unappreciated. Two significant things came out about this. First, she wanted acknowledgement for how clean she kept the house, and second, she didn't feel like her husband was very emotionally available. Tom thought Sara kept the house clean because it was important to *her* and it had nothing to do with him. He felt if it was important to Sara (and not to him), and if Sara was doing it for herself, then he didn't need to make a point to say anything.

"Do you like having the house clean, the way she keeps it?" I asked Tom.

"Oh, yeah," he answered. "It's not that I prefer things messy. I just don't feel like I have to clean before I do anything else, like she does."

"Here is the authenticity piece," I said. "If you appreciate the clean house, then share with her how much you appreciate it. In doing that, you are simply telling the truth about how you feel. Plus, Sara needs to hear it." As soon as I said that, Sara started crying.

"But I don't want her to start thinking I *expect* it," Tom replied. "That's why I don't really say anything. I don't want her to think I am one of those guys who thinks that cleaning is 'women's work.'"

"I know you don't expect it," Sara interjected. "Some men expect their women to do everything, and I know you don't. I just want to feel like you care about me."

"Would you be okay with me telling you every day that the place looks nice and that I love you?" Tom asked.

"Before you answer that," I interrupted, "How would it be for you to tell Sara every day that the house looks nice, and then also show her some affection and tell her how you feel about her? How does that sit with you?"

"That would be great, if I remember," Tom said. "Really, I am afraid she is just going to push me away most of the time if I try." His head sank and he began to look really sad.

"Sara," I asked, "would you be okay with Tom telling you every day how good the house looks and how much he appreciates your effort?"

"I don't even need it every day," she answered. "Well, maybe every day for the first week, then just twice a week from then on," she added, smiling.

"So Tom," I added, "if there was a pretty good chance Sara wasn't going to push you away, you would do it?"

"Well, yeah," he responded. "It's just that she operates on the half-mile rule." He was deflecting with humor.

"I do not!" Sara protested with a smile and smack on his arm.

"What is the half-mile rule?" I asked.

"She can't have sex if there is clutter in anyone's house within a half-mile," he answered jokingly. We all laughed for a second.

"So, again," I asked, "how would it be to tell Sara every day that you appreciate having a clean house?"

"I do appreciate it,"Tom said, turning to his wife. "You do an incredible job and you seem to do it effortlessly. It's wonderful. Thank you."

"And how would it be to grab her while she is cleaning every once in a while and hug her and tell her she has to stop for 15 seconds and feel how much you love her?" I asked.

"When she is cleaning, she is like a tornado," he said. "I will do it, but if she hits me, I am coming after you, dude." He then turned back to her and mouthed, *I love you*.

You can see in this dialogue how some of our feelings about our relationships can get projected onto our feelings about housework. In this case, Sara was frustrated about Tom's lack of affection and Tom was afraid to show any affection because he was scared Sara would reject him personally.

Sara acknowledged shortly after this that she was really willing to work on letting Tom's love in before the house is clean. She also shared that she didn't feel like anyone *could* love her until the house is clean and how genuinely confusing it is to have him express affection before she is finished cleaning. Sara took responsibility for not only pushing Tom away, but also for demanding acknowledgement for cleaning because in her house growing up, she felt as though cleaning was the only thing that made her worthy.

"I don't mind taking care of things for you; I want to support you. But if you don't care about me, I can't do this anymore." When Lizzie said this to her husband Pete, it shocked and scared him—and it brought their argument about housework to a screeching halt. Pete was stunned. They continued to talk after the argument, but Pete never asked Lizzie to clarify her statement and Lizzie never asked Pete what he had heard that made his face go pale. The more they talked, the more frustrated Lizzie got because she felt more and more used and unappreciated. The angrier Lizzie got, the more scared Pete got.

It took some digging to identify this statement of Lizzie's as the turning point in the whole argument. She meant one thing, he heard another. Lizzie meant that if he didn't show some appreciation for all the housework that she did, she would not continue to do so much to support him. Like the woman in the previous example, Lizzie had self-worth issues and taking care of everything at home was how she felt validated. While she really enjoyed the life that she had, she wanted to be honored and acknowledged for all she did—and especially for all of the things she took care of to support her husband in his business.

What Pete heard is that he had neglected his wife by pouring so much of himself into his business and that Lizzie felt taken advantage of and now wanted a divorce. This started a cascade of fatalistic doubt and shame in him. He began wondering if he should have even started his business and if it had become so big and so all consuming that he didn't even notice that he had lost his wife in the process.

"I knew that I was working a lot and that I haven't been as available to her the last couple of years," Pete said. "But I didn't know it had gotten *this* bad." He hadn't shared that that was how he had taken Lizzie's statement that she couldn't do this anymore. So Pete was scared that Lizzie was filing for divorce while Lizzie was angry because she thought Pete was being overly dramatic about the threat of losing her free labor as his personal assistant.

Once they cleared up this misunderstanding and Pete realized that his wife did not want a divorce, he started crying almost uncontrollably. "Honey, I couldn't make it a day without you," he said. "I mean, you know, I would make it—but it would suck so bad! Nothing I do would have any meaning. The only way I have been able to achieve what I have is because I have had your support. Please don't ever take that away from me. Please tell me what I can do to support *you*."

"What would you *like* to do to show Lizzie how much she means to you and to thank her for everything she does for you?" I asked.

"Well, just yesterday, I was thinking about getting my sister to come hang with the kids for four days," Pete answered. "Then we could go hiking in the mountains together for four days straight. I want to go do that with you," he said, looking at his wife.

"You hate hiking," she responded.

"Yeah, but I love *you,* and we are long overdue for a vacation together," he responded. "I just want to have the time to stay wrapped up in you and not worry about anything else except keeping up with you as you run up some damn mountain."

Pete wanted to do more for his wife and for his marriage. He felt like he needed to do something tangible to show his appreciation because he had become so busy over the last several years that he felt that his words had become empty to Lizzie. His wife was more than willing to accept his offer.

"I can live without the hiking trip, but I can't live feeling unappreciated," she said. "I am gonna hold you to that hiking trip now that you have said it out loud. I have a witness," she added, wagging a playful finger at him.

Lizzie's work in this was to voice her frustrations when they were minor irritations and not let them snowball to the point where she began to resent Pete. Pete's work was to learn how to be mindful of every time that his wife did something for him and to acknowledge it by feeling his love, gratitude, and appreciation—and then expressing that to her.

"Why do we always have to do things *your* way?" Zoe, the client who said this, spoke these words in a whiny voice. She had played the part of the victim for a good portion of her life and was constantly frustrated that she never let her strength show in her really important relationships.

Zoe's husband George tried to rule the house through intimidation and insults. Whenever Zoe began to change how she did things to meet her own needs, George would yell at her, chastise her, threaten divorce, or make very passive-aggressive attempts to subvert her changes.

One day, Zoe wanted to move all the dishes from one kitchen cabinet to the cabinet closest to the stove where food was prepared. "George threw a fit!" she told me. "He took every plate out of the cabinet and put it on the kitchen table where I was working on a big sewing project for our daughter. When I walked back in the kitchen, he started yelling from the living room, 'I decided to move the dishes to make it work better. I guess I should have asked you first, huh?'" She put the dishes back in the cabinet by the stove only to find them on the kitchen table again the next day. This continued for three days before she came into my office for her weekly session.

Zoe shared several stories about how she had constantly been held down emotionally and treated as if her voice and her desires didn't matter. Although she had done a lot of healing work before she began her sessions with me, she had never been able to get over this hump.

"When I get home, the dishes will probably be on the table again," she said. "Yesterday, he even emptied the Tupperware cabinet onto the table."

"Any idea why George was so triggered?" I asked.

"No. I just keep asking him why we have to do it his way. He says that his way is better. That's all he will say."

While we were talking, I kept thinking of smart-ass ways that Zoe could turn George's power struggle back on him.

"There is a rule about getting into a power struggle with teenagers," I told her. "It applies to adults, too. *Never get into a power struggle you can't win.* So let me ask you this first. Do you feel safe physically? Would George ever hurt you or hit you no matter how mad he got?"

"He would never lay a hand on me," she answered.

"Does he have a sense of humor?" I asked.

"Oh, yeah. A great one—when he's not mad at me!" Zoe said. "We are always playing practical jokes on each other. Big ones!"

"When someone gets the best of him, will he give in and admit that he was bested?" I asked.

"He will stew about it for a couple of days, but then I will hear him telling the story to someone and loving it."

I next threw out a suggestion about how Zoe might approach things differently so as not to feel powerless. She had never considered bringing her sharp wit into play in troubled situations. I wanted to bridge the gap between the powerful, smart-ass woman she could be and the whiny victim she turned into when her husband yelled at her. After asking her a bunch of questions, I came up with a plan.

"Ok, here's what you do," I told her. "But remember—if you can't do this with a lot of love, it won't work." Zoe nodded and I continued. "Empty the cabinet and just have a bare cabinet with only a stack of paper plates. Put all the real dishes on *his* side of the bed. Cook a good dinner and serve it on the paper plates. If he asks why, just tell him you didn't want to fight about the plates anymore, and don't say anything else about it. If George keeps pushing, tell him you are exhausted and are headed to bed. When George walks in the room later and finds all the dishes on the bed, pull out a squirt gun and blast him as you keep screaming, 'I moved the dishes. I guess I should have asked you first.'"

Zoe carried out the plan almost to the letter, adding an inflatable woman to the scene in the bed with the plates and hiding herself in the closet. When George walked in, he yelled, "What in the hell is this?" Zoe came out of the closet and started blasting him with a giant water cannon she bought just for the occasion. George yelled at her for another couple of seconds, and then he stopped. "Okay, okay, you win!" he said, laughing. He melted and dropped his head. Zoe just smiled.

She dropped the water cannon on the bed and slowly walked over to him, flashing her best "come hither" grin. She put her hands on George's water-soaked waist and said with a soft, compassionate, yet firm voice, "Sweetie, I am going to decide where we keep the dishes. Otherwise, we will be having prank wars forever and you will lose *as usual*." She kissed him and he kissed her back. After that, Zoe felt different being in the house with him. She had a glimpse of what it could be like when she did not go to her victim place when he started to bully her verbally.

While this story perhaps should come with a "Don't try this at home" disclaimer, it shows how our deepest emotional issues play out in our home life. George had an overbearing mother who had constantly emasculated him whenever he tried to step up to be the man of the house after his father died when George was 12. He played out this wound by being overbearing himself and trying to make it seem as if everything that happened in the house was *his* idea. This went against his normally kind, tenderhearted nature because as with all wounds that we don't heal, they come out in the most annoying ways.

For her part, Zoe grew up with an overbearing father who kept his tender heart buried under layers of anger. She had been the class clown and would do comedy shows for her mother, while her father never appreciated her humor. No matter how hard she tried, she could never please her father or do anything good enough to gain his approval. This played out in her adult life as her hiding her witty sarcastic side from George whenever he was critical of her.

Over time, Zoe continued to set boundaries with George in similar ways whenever he resisted her attempts to balance their power dynamic. Now, she only has to *threaten* to get out the water cannon; she doesn't have to actually use it!

"I couldn't believe he *expected* me to have sex after he had just *expected* me to take over keeping the whole damn house clean." This example deals with a specific incidence where sex and housework got confused and the couple went from being upset at the start of the session, to the husband feeling deep despair in the middle of the session, to the two of them barely making it home with their clothes on because they couldn't wait to have sex.

During a two-week period where Doug had to work 13- to 16-hour days, six days a week, to cover for a co-worker who was on vacation, he and his wife Tonya agreed that he would not cook or vacuum during that time. Doug had asked her really nicely about this a few days ahead of time, and Tonya said she didn't mind picking up the extra responsibility.

During the second week, Doug started falling asleep on the couch watching television after dinner. Each night, he had taken off his pants, socks, and shoes before falling asleep on the couch. At some point during the night, he would wake up and go to bed. The next morning when he dressed and went to work, he'd leave his pants and socks from the previous day on the living room floor. By the third day this happened, Tonya was feeling taken advantage of. It wasn't her responsibility to pick up his clothes, she thought, and she was still making dinner each night and doing all of the dishes. A couple of nights, she had even put the kids to bed all by herself.

On the fourth night of the second week, Doug woke up on the couch while Tonya was just going to bed. He came into the bedroom and started kissing her, clearly wanting to initiate sex. *He has turned into a slob, leaving me to do everything, and now he wants sex!* Tanya thought to herself. She felt like all the responsibility for keeping the house together was now on her. She felt as though if she had sex with Doug, it would have been telling him that it was okay for him to leave his dirty clothes on the living room floor. So she didn't respond favorably to his advances.

"Did you pick up your clothes and your cups from the living room?" she asked, essentially shutting down his advances. "I almost couldn't get into the bathroom this morning when I got up to shower because you left your shirt on the floor."

"She had one of those tones in her voice that let me know there was no way we were going to have sex," Doug shared when they came to my office the following Tuesday. "I knew she was upset about something and I was too tired to try and figure out what it was. I just rolled over and went to sleep. It wasn't until two days later that I was even conscious enough to ask about it after sleeping in on my day off. I still don't understand what got her so mad."

"I couldn't believe he *expected* me to have sex after he had just *expected* me to take over keeping the whole damn house clean," Tonya said, agitated.

"It wasn't that I *expected* you to have sex with me. I *wanted* to have sex with you. There's a difference," Doug responded.

"What's the difference?" Tonya demanded to know.

He looked at her for a split second with his mouth open, as if he were about to say something, then shook his head, looking disappointed. "Forget it," he said. "I guess there's not a difference." He stared at the floor, looking as if the wind had been taken out of his sails. She already had her arms crossed, but she pulled them a tiny bit tighter across her heart and turned her head to look away

"Stop for a second," I said. "Stay with that Doug. What's the difference between *expecting* her to have sex and *wanting* to have sex with her?"

"I don't know. I guess there isn't any," he said, looking defeated.

"You look really sad," I said.

"It's just . . . I don't know . . . I thought we were doing better." Then he turned to Tonya and said, "I guess I didn't realize what it was like for you. I am sorry. I really don't want it to feel that way. I thought . . . I am . . . I am sorry." As he spoke, he started to tear up.

"You thought we were doing better because I was willing to do all the cleaning around the house?" Tonya asked, as if she couldn't believe what she was hearing.

"No," he said before pausing with his mouth open, looking confused, searching for the words. "I thought we were doing better because I thought you knew how much I loved you and I thought you felt the same way. I didn't realize that sex was like a chore for you. I had no idea. I just . . . I am sorry." He started sobbing gently.

Tonya looked shocked. The stunned look on her face said, *Wait, what?*

I asked Doug how he was feeling. He shook his head slightly and made an *It doesn't matter* expression. He looked like he was dying inside.

"Doug, what's going on inside you right now?" I asked. "Take a breath and let yourself feel it."

He shook his head again. "I'm an idiot," he told me. Turning again to Tonya, he added, "I know I was more tired than any human being should ever have to be last week. I felt like the walking dead. I am sorry I wasn't able to help out around the house. I felt like all I was doing was cleaning up messes all day at work. I didn't realize how hard it was going to be; I really was working two full-time jobs. I was also really missing you. By that Thursday, I felt like I hadn't seen you in a week and a half, so I tried to stay up and that is why I came to bed right when you did. I just wanted to connect with you, but I didn't know."

"Do you guys realize that you are talking about two different subjects?" I asked. "Doug, you are talking about sex. Tonya, you have been talking about housework." They both looked confused.

"Tonya, go back to when he started kissing on you Thursday night," I suggested. "Did you want to have sex with Doug?" I asked.

"Well, yeah. I did, but I didn't know what to do. I was worried that he wouldn't ever pick up or help around the house again." Turning to him, she added, "I was pretty tired, too. I was a little freaked out by how far gone you were and how much I had to do when you weren't helping out."

"Does sex feel like a chore for you?" I asked her.

"No. Where are you guys getting that?" she asked, exasperated.

"Doug is over here dying inside because after shutting him down Thursday night, you said a few minutes ago that there wasn't any difference between him expecting you to have sex and him wanting to have sex with you," I explained. "He took that to mean that you only have sex with him out of obligation and that you don't have any real desire to be with him sexually."

Doug perked up, feeling as though someone finally understood how he was feeling.

"What? No honey," Tonya replied. "I love being with you. That's not even close! It's just the opposite."

"What did you mean when you said that there isn't any difference between him *expecting* you to have sex and *wanting* to have sex with you?" I asked.

"I didn't mean anything by it. I was mad and freaked out because I felt all alone at home last week," she explained. "You were like a zombie, but I guess I didn't realize how bad it was until now. I was getting to the point where I was ready to have sex with you in your sleep, but I just freaked. I am sorry."

"What could you guys have each said or done to avoid this whole thing?" I asked.

Neither of them had any idea.

"How about this," I offered. "When Doug started trying to get freaky with you on Thursday night, what if you had said, 'I have been wanting to schtoink you all week and I have gotten scared that even after you finish this hard two weeks at work that I will get stuck still doing all the housework.' How does that sound, Tonya?"

"Yeah, that's how I really felt," she said. "Why didn't I just say that?"

"Or what if you kissed him really hard and said, 'If a week goes by after your schedule gets back to normal, and I am still the only one doing all the housework, I am gonna kick your ass and you are never gonna get laid again," I suggested. Doug laughed out loud and then sat there grinning.

Tonya laughed at first, and then she said to me, "I wouldn't ever say that to him."

"No, honey, that would work," Doug interjected. "I think I would rather hear *that* than what you actually said at the time."

"Really?" she asked with a smile. "Okay."

"Try it now," I said. "Look him in the eye. Say, 'I have been wanting to get freaky with you all week. And I want you to know that if another week goes by and I am still the only one doing the housework, I am going to kick your ass and you aren't gonna get laid ever again." Her eyes were dancing as she looked at him and repeated the words.

"Deal," he said as they smiled at each other.

Later, Doug sent me a text message saying that Tonya was all over him in the car on the way home and that she had begged him to take the rest of the day off so they could spend the next four hours alone together before their children got home from school.

What Does It Take?

To have a fight about housework, one or both people have to have some kind of buried hurt or fear that that is leaking out in a bad way. Sometimes, the issue begins with a mere difference in expectations; resolving this can be a simple matter. However, when couples combine different expectations with a poor way of responding internally to those expectations, they end up with a recipe for disaster. How they respond to their feelings and to each other will ultimately determine the quality of their relationship.

Arguing and tension around housework is an indicator that they have strong expectations that are failing to be met in some way. What they need to communicate is what is going on inside for each of them when their expectations aren't met. Most couples with housework issues either have little awareness about their own opinions of the way it's supposed to be or they feel completely justified in having those opinions.

What cracks me up is when people who normally are very good about owning their own feelings and expressing themselves appropriately with their partner suddenly come out with a zinger that is dripping with blame or shame or that sets a manipulative trap, acting as if the virtue of taking emotional responsibility only applies to the *rest* of our lives, not to housework. These people will then get triggered further when their partners object to what they are saying. Often, the partner is objecting to the perceived judgment instead of to the words his or her beloved is using.

Who Does What Around the House

Gender stereotypes paint a picture that men are slobs and women are responsible for picking up after them. This notion still prevails in a lot of households, although I see many couples who do not fit this stereotype at all. Plenty of men do most of the housework and are frustrated that their women are not as neat and tidy as they want them to be.

Some couples just clean whatever they want whenever they want. This works best when both people have similar tolerance levels. With other couples, each person is responsible for keeping a different part of the house clean. Sometimes she is responsible for picking up dishes and clothes and he is responsible for vacuuming and cleaning the bathroom. Or maybe he cooks and she washes dishes after the meal. Even then, however, issues still come up about one person not doing his or her assigned duties—especially when that person believes special circumstances apply and the other doesn't see it quite that way.

No matter what the specific situation or division of duties, what determines whether a couple will have issues about housework is how each of them responds internally when one notices something that needs to be done that hasn't registered on the other's radar. When I notice just a few dishes in the sink and I don't like it, for example, I have to take responsibility for my own discomfort. My discomfort is not my wife's responsibility; my discomfort is my responsibility! I do this by cleaning whatever I notice needs to be cleaned.

This came up the other day when I was stretching on our bedroom floor and saw the carpet was dirty. Instead of thinking, *Why hasn't my wife vacuumed?* I thought, *Wow! How did I not notice this? I am going to get the vacuum cleaner.* When my wife came home, she thanked me for vacuuming. I didn't do it for her, I did it for myself because I wanted the floor to be clean *and* it still felt great to have my small effort appreciated.

The bottom line is that we always have the responsibility for creating our half of the relationship. We are responsible for how we communicate.

PRACTICES:

- Sit down with your partner when both of you are feeling close and you are not arguing. Take turns completing the following sentences: "When the house is messy, I feel _____ and it means that I am _____." When the house is clean, I feel _____ and it means that I am _____."

- Walk around the house together, with each of you saying what pleases you and displeases you about what you see at that very moment, with the house being exactly the way it is. Resist the urge to clean anything as you walk around together. Notice if you get triggered at any point.

- Make a list of the things each of you wants to see changed around the house. Divide the list between short-term tasks that can reasonably be finished in the next 24 hours and tasks that can reasonably be done over the next week. Don't include any longer-term projects. Together, come up with a plan for attacking the list that both of you feel good about. Pay particular attention to whether or not you begin to feel a sense of urgency or a sense of wanting to please the other person. Aim for a plan that feels relaxed and that you can decide upon with an easy-going cooperative communication.

CHAPTER 14

INSPIRING YOUR MAN VS. EMASCULATING YOUR MAN

Let's be honest. Your man is going to disappoint you in some way. It's going to happen. He is going to do something stupid or insensitive, and it is not going to happen just once—he is going to screw up for the rest of his life. Sometimes he will do something thoughtless by accident; sometimes he will do something stupid intentionally (even though he knows better).

He's going to be watching sports or playing on the computer instead of helping you do something that requires his help. He is going to forget your birthday or your anniversary. He's going to talk to that good-looking woman at the party longer than you want him to, or he's going to make an inappropriate joke at the worst possible time. He's going to work too late and ruin date night. He's going to spend money on something that you don't think he needs and maybe can't afford in the first place. You can count on at least some of these things happening. We have a technical term for all that. It's called *being human*. We all do it. We all make mistakes.

So when your man has dropped the ball, hurt your feelings, and once again proven that he's an idiot, what do you do? You have two options: *love* or *fear*. Acting out of one will inspire him, while acting out of the other will emasculate him. You get to choose.

ACCEPTING HIS MISTAKES

I'm willing to bet that part of what you fell in love with when you fell in love with your man was the man he *could be* because you saw the *potential* in him. You want him to become the man that you know he can be—and when you are frustrated with him, you want him to be that man *right now*!

Maybe you want him to do more housework but he's oblivious; maybe you see that he could be more successful in his career and something is holding him back; maybe you want to feel more emotional intimacy and he keeps the volume on his feelings turned way down. Whatever it is, you want something from him and he is not giving it to you.

Few other people are in a stronger position than you are to inspire him to be the man he is capable of being. After all, you know him better than anyone else, love him more than anyone else, and see him at his best and at his worst. If you are *not* an inspiration to him and if you do *not* feel like an incredible source of support to him, what's getting in the way? Before you can inspire your man, you have to *accept* him—just as he is, right now—and then you have to *communicate* that to him.

Wishing he were different than he is will only put you on the path to frustration. Acceptance is the path to growth. If your man is not being the man he is capable of being, living the life he is capable of living, and supporting you the way you need to be supported, he is probably lacking in some way in confidence and self-worth. He needs your acceptance; he needs your vision of who he can be. And he probably *won't* or *can't* tell you how badly he needs your support, acceptance, and inspiration because acknowledging that would leave him feeling too vulnerable for his comfort.

Your man may never have had a model to follow of an emotionally strong man with an open heart. Most men are taught that having an open heart leads to weakness. Because of this, your man is probably not as emotionally strong as he wants to be. That's why he needs you to hold that vision for him, and possibly also hold him accountable—but in a *loving, supportive* way.

So how do you accept him as he is and, at the same time, want him to grow into the potential you envision for him? You do it the same way you address behaviors with a child—separate his worth from his behavior. Accept and affirm the man first, before you begin to address the behavior you want him to change.

Start by really feeling your love for him and your desire to be with him. Take your time to get in touch with this, and let it fill you up. Once you are really feeling your love and your desire, then it's time to talk to your man and communicate his worth. Remind him *repeatedly* that HE is the guy you want to be with and HE is the man you love. He needs to hear this from you! He really does! He is an awesome and capable man, and if you leave this part out, he may not be able to hear the rest of what you have to say.

You may need to affirm this 80 percent of the time and address the behaviors that need changing only 20 percent of the time, or maybe it will take you saying ten likable and supportive things before he will be able to hear the one thing you want to address. We all need to hear what we are doing that *is* working before we can hear what we are doing that isn't working—and this is even *more* important for people who have low self-esteem or who are frustrated with their lives in some way. Leading the discussion with the positive will set your man up for success.

COMPLAINING KILLS PASSION

Acceptance takes being present and employing deliberate focus and effort. Some women's default, on the other hand, is complaining—a major sign that that they're playing the part of the victim. Complaining is *not* going to motivate your guy to be a better man. It's going to motivate him to get you to shut up. (That may sound harsh, and I am not interested in pulling any punches when it comes to helping people create awesome relationships.)

If you respond out of fear instead of love and resort to complaining instead of acceptance, you will pay a hefty price. He's going to shut down, resent you, and argue back, and it's going to fuel the tension between you. That tension, over time, is what kills true passion. When his passion for you is gone and resentment reigns, he won't feel safe to open his heart to you. And the only level of sexual passion he will share is the physical release he gets from having sex with you.

Women often object that their man's behavior has already killed *their* passion, so what's the point? I totally understand. Nobody gets hot and bothered over a man with his head up his ass. And you have to understand a very important principle: His disappointing you does not give you a license to play victim. Even if he is an idiot, you are still required to step up and take responsibility for your own feelings. If you want things to be better, you have to take action and do your part to make them better. He may not have the emotional sophistication you want him to have, so you may have to be patient with him and teach him. You may have to be the one who leads the way toward building the relationship that you want. It probably already has many good elements that you can build on, and your work may be just a matter of filling in the gaps between the two of you that have opened up over the years.

If you take responsibility for your own feelings, he will be more likely to hear you, to take your feelings into account, and to feel and share his own feelings. If you do *not* take responsibility for your feelings in communicating with him, I guarantee that he will not open up to you more. Taking responsibility for your own feelings is *never* a bad option.

I know what you're thinking. *This all makes sense, but it isn't so easy in the heat of the moment. What do I do when I get triggered? How can I possibly* not *complain?* One of the most effective techniques for going from complaining (fear) to acceptance (love) is something called stepping in. Just softening your face and physically moving closer to him can be a powerful symbol of acceptance. Stepping in is *not* the same thing as not backing away. It's *embracing* the situation by being willing to feel every aspect of your experience in the moment and being the accepting embodiment of love.

Stepping in also means not getting dismayed by the fact that a problem has come up, and instead seeing the problem as a chance to get closer. By becoming more fully present and not emotionally running away to a place of dramatic victimization, stubborn resentment, wits-end frustration, or scorch-the-earth anger, you can instead confront your man from a place of calm acceptance. By feeling your desire to be closer to him and communicating that desire, you're being caring instead of critical. Again, he needs you to care about him and communicate your desire, even if he is too proud to allow himself to be vulnerable enough to say it.

Time Out

If despite your best efforts to be loving and accepting, you still want to run over your man with a tank, there is no point in talking to him right then. All it will do is create resistance in him and he will not be able to hear what you have to say. Until you get to a place of acceptance, don't say anything more than, "Honey, I love you and I am so pissed off at you, right now. If we discuss this now, I am going to be really bitchy. So I am going to go chill out for a second. I will be back when I am able to love you and I don't want to snuff you out." Then go do whatever you have to do to get back into a place of feeling love.

If you need to go scream or cry, do it! If you need to call a girlfriend or go for a walk, do it! If you need to journal for a few minutes or do yoga, do it! Just make sure you *breathe!* (You might also try doing a loving kindness meditation or the loving visualization from Chapter 4.) As Albert Einstein said, "A problem cannot be solved with the same level of thinking that created it." This is the time to reconnect with your own spirit, to ask for help and say a meditative prayer, and to raise your vibration. Some call this finding your center. Rhonda Byrne, author of *The Secret*, refers to it as "getting yourself onto the feeling frequency of love." Whatever you call it, you need to find that quiet place inside where you can let go of your judgments and *trust* that a full resolution to the problem is possible.

How to Communicate That You Are Disappointed and Still Accept Him

One time I bought oversized exhaust for my truck. (That's a larger, high-performance, cooler-looking set of exhaust pipes.) I had not told my wife about it, and when I got home from work a couple of days later, a very large box that was too big to miss was sitting by the front door. My wife asked what was in the box and I started justifying as a way of deflecting (a tactic of my father's that I saw modeled growing up).

"I noticed this auction on eBay late the other night. You had already gone to bed. The auction was about to end and no one had bid on it at all. It was for a brand new oversized exhaust for the truck. It will lower the exhaust gas temperature and ultimately extend the life of the truck. I priced it at the muffler shop for over $650. But I got it on eBay for $187. I saved more money by not getting the ceramic coated down tube, which would have been another $200." I didn't include the additional $50 for shipping in the price I reported to her.

My wife, being the jewel that she is, dropped her head laughing, started shaking her head, and said, "I love how excited you get about stuff for your truck. You are so funny and this really is something you should have told me about ahead of time. This is the kind of stuff that scares me." She was right of course, I should have told her. We were struggling financially at the time. I had just finished graduate school, I didn't have a lot of therapy clients yet, and my horseshoeing business was not even paying the bills. What struck me was her acceptance of me. Her acceptance affirmed my worth. She was understandably annoyed, and she didn't let her annoyance get in the way of her adoring me.

Feeling her acceptance of me, I could also feel how bad it felt to disappoint her. This created a far greater change in me than if she had shamed me or nagged me. If she had taken that route, I would have just tried harder to hide things better in the future. Her handling it this way instead made me *want* to communicate with her and not hide anything and it inspired me to be a more mature partner financially.

If your message is not palatable to your man, there is no point in delivering it. When he is not listening, you are wasting your time and energy talking to him. If he senses that you are shaming, blaming, or putting him down, he will argue with you or shut you out.

Tell him that you really want him to hear what you have to say. If he still is not able to hear you, then either your message is still not palatable to him or he may just need to talk for a while to get through his stuff before he can listen. If listening and really hearing you is too much for him and affirming him never softens his resistance to being vulnerable with you, then you may have to make some hard decisions about whether or not you want to stay in the relationship. But I guarantee that you aren't even close to having to make that decision right now, even though it may be the only solution you can think of.

WHY MEN LIE

In Chapter 8, I mentioned how women can sense inauthenticity in men because they can sense a man's emotional state. When your man is saying one thing and you sense something else in him, you will feel it. He may not even be aware of it (most of the time he won't be), but you will feel it. You may not be 100 percent accurate in your perception of it; you may not get the content of what's going on inside him right, but you will feel the discord between his words and his feelings. You can tell when he's not being completely authentic and completely genuine. You will sense that you cannot trust what he is saying and he will not feel safe to you.

This is *not* necessarily cause for alarm; it just means that the two of you have some discovery to do. Men often draw the conclusion that it is *not* okay to tell the truth some of the time. We get the message through life experiences that if we tell the whole truth, it creates problems—and men don't want problems any more than women do.

What often ends up happening is we try to tell as much of the truth as we think our women can hear without having a big emotional reaction. We are terrified of your emotional reactions! There is nothing actually wrong with your passionate emotional storms—in fact we love them (when they are not directed at us). Just understand that they scare the crap out of us! No matter how big, strong, tough, or accomplished a man is, inside of every man lives a little boy who is still afraid of Mommy being mad at him.

So we lie a little or hold back the whole truth to hide something we know we shouldn't have done or because we think the truth would scare you and we genuinely think that you have no real reason to be scared. We do this not only to try to keep the peace, but also to keep the focus away from our areas of insecurity. The only problem with lying like this is that emotional intimacy suffers. We know that you sense when we are lying, but like idiots, we just keep hoping that we can lie well enough to satisfy you.

When you sense that your man is lying to you, it is an opportunity to help him be a bigger man. This requires you to have confidence not only in yourself, but also in the relationship. It requires you to have faith in the communication process you are learning in this book and in the vision you have of the man who your man is capable of being.

This is also an opportunity for you to be a bigger woman. If you choose to be the biggest woman you can be, you can use this tuning-fork awareness to open a door for your man and to broaden his awareness. Your man is not going to take the initiative to call himself on his own BS. He is probably not even aware that he is not telling the whole truth. Since you have this awareness, it is *your* responsibly to trust your instinct, to trust what your body is telling you, and take the lead in sharing your awareness with him. (Just remember, your tuning-fork awareness—no matter how accurate—is not a license to skip over acceptance.)

This ability to sense what is going on inside your man is a gift, and gifts come with responsibilities. This gift was given to you to keep you safe and to help you propel your relationships into deeper intimacy through authenticity. It was not given to you to be a burden, nor to be a weapon. Not speaking up and not honoring your own awareness is a sure-fire way to make your awareness feel like a burden. Both feeling burdened by your keen awareness and using it as a weapon are paths to the dark side. Stay away from the dark side! If you nag your man, accuse him of lying, or shame him, he will fight you. It is imperative that you accept that he is doing the best he can. Chances are he's just not up to speed with the whole *authenticity* thing yet.

When your man is hiding something, the story he's telling is coming out of his own issues and the need he feels to defend himself. While he is talking, you feel like you can't trust him, and your nervous system is screaming *run!* Your own story starts to play in your head, and it sounds something like this: *He doesn't love me. If he did, he would have the balls to tell me the truth. I can't trust him. How could I be so stupid as to believe that he ever loved me?* This is the voice of *fear*, not the voice of *love*.

The voice of love says, "Hey sweetie, I hear what you are saying and I get it, *and* I feel like there is this whole other part that isn't being talked about and I don't know what it is. When you are ready to share the rest of it, I want to hear it." If you say something like this while accepting him and feeling your desire to be close to him, and he feels your acceptance, one of two things will happen. Either he will relish the opportunity to share the larger and deeper truth or he will stick with his story, continue to lie, and try to convince you that he *did* tell you the whole truth by attempting to back up his original story.

If he shares more, be patient with him; he is forging a new path and it is going to be slow navigating what is undiscovered territory for him. Thank him and celebrate that he is sharing with you, even if you don't like the content of what he is saying. Don't start arguing with him. Encourage him to keep sharing by listening and asking questions to keep him talking.

If he defends his lie and denies that he has anything more to share, don't argue. You don't have to convince him that you are right. Instead, have confidence and trust your feelings that there is more to discover. Accept the fact that he is *not* ready to share it right now. It's frustrating, but if he is not ready, then he is not ready. Keep accepting him—and don't freak out.

THE IMPORTANCE OF NOT FREAKING OUT

Your man may need to experience you *not* freaking out before he feels like he is ready to share more. At some point in his life, this man of yours has had some woman freak out on him (or maybe *a lot* of women freaking out on him). Maybe it was you, maybe it was an ex-wife or ex-girlfriend, or maybe it was his mom. Whoever it was, chances are that he is willing to do almost anything to avoid another freak-out scene. If you get scared, attack him, or get dramatic when you sense that he isn't telling you the whole story, he may take that as an indicator that it is not safe to share more. Should he tell you the truth anyway? *Yes, he should.* Is he ready to do that? *Maybe not.*

Instead of freaking out, try getting curious. Curiosity is probably the most underrated feeling in our culture. It carries the spiritual energy of childlike innocence. Curiosity is the path to wisdom because it keeps our awareness fresh and our nerves calm. Feeling "certain," on the other hand, kills our awareness because it flips on the "no vacancy" sign, turning anything new away at the door.

When you sense your man is holding back with you or holding back in his life, *get curious!* Get curious about how he sees his world. Ask him simple questions, and listen to the answers. Ask him questions that follow what he has said. Ask him questions that have nothing to do with your opinion. Ask him what he likes, ask him what he doesn't like, even if it doesn't make sense to you. Every now and then, ask him how something feels when it is happening. The bottom line is that having someone in your life who gets curious about you feels good. Coming from a place of curiosity implies acceptance. Wanting to understand his world will help him feel heard. When he feels heard, honored, and respected, then he will be ready to hear your different opinion in return.

WHY ME?

You may be thinking, *Why do I have to be the one to hold space for him? Why do I have to do all the work?* I want you to recognize the victim's voice in that question. Asking this question is *whining*. And the whiny victim will try to block the powerful woman-warrior *every time*. Is that *really* what you want for yourself? If it isn't, then take a minute right now to write down what that victim voice is saying, and then write down the inspired response to that voice. You may well be ready for the responsibility of taking your life to a whole other level—you may recognize the voice of God inside you, calling you to be more and to stand more fully in your power.

The reason *you* have to be the one to hold space and do the work (at least at first) is because *you* are the one with more awareness about what is going on with this particular issue, and the alternative is destructive complaining, nagging, or henpecking. Henpecking is a way of getting him to just barely do enough to shut you up. Inspiring your man to be everything he's capable of being doesn't really take any more effort than complaining and has a much better payoff. It requires a lot, though—faith in love, faith in the communication process, patience, and confidence in yourself. If that seems like too much to ask, imagine what it will be like to live the rest of your life complaining, nagging, and resenting. Which life would you rather be living 20 years from now?

RESPONSIBILITY OF MEN IN RELATIONSHIPS

I have not talked about what your man has to do. That's a whole other subject. In fact, it is a whole other book. I recommend that you and your partner listen to "The New Man" podcast by men's coach Tripp Lanier (www.thenewmanpodcast.com/more/about-the-new-man), or read psychotherapist Jayson Gaddis's blog, "Awakening Through Life, Relationships and Parenting" (http://www.jaysongaddis.com). Suggest your man inquire about The Mankind Project (mankindproject.org) or the Authentic Man Program (www.authenticmanprogram.com), or suggest he read *Way of the Superior Man* by David Deada. All of these sources and thousands of others are directed to get men to step up on their own. They are powerful programs created to support and guide men in doing their own growth work. The men aren't getting off scot-free—far from it. They just aren't the ones for whom this chapter was written.

This entire chapter is about talking women into living up to their potential as strong, powerful, insightful women. Women, you need to step up and demand more of us men. It is time for you to stop letting us get by with our insecure, big-ego ways of avoiding emotional responsibility. When we are being closed-off jerks, be willing to call us on our defensive deflection tactics and take responsibility for what you know. If it comes to it, walk away if you need to. If every woman in the world decided to set a higher standard and walk away from men who do not measure up emotionally, the men of the world would take it as a wake-up call and step up the learning curve. (Either that, or we would all become homosexual; either way, you would be better off.)

But before you think about walking away, first try mastering the emotional and communication skills in this book, practicing acceptance, and learning to inspire your man to be the man he is capable of being. It is an incredible challenge to remain hopeful and to keep your faith in your man's heart. But I have faith in you—if you've read this far in the book, then I know you can do this!

PRACTICES:

- Think of a time that your man has frustrated you. Describe what he did or how he was acting. Now think of a time when you did the same thing or acted the same way. Your defensive mind may say, *I have never done that, I would never treat anyone that way.* But chances are you have done something similar. Even if you haven't done the same exact thing, you have probably hurt someone just as badly (even if you didn't want to or mean to). If you remember doing something that hurt someone even though you didn't think what you did was wrong, feel compassion for the other person's pain and accept yourself even though you played a part in that person's pain. The goal is to eventually develop acceptance for your man when he hurts you or frustrates you.

- Create an image in your mind of your man fulfilling his potential. Hold that image of him as you feel your feelings of loving him. Feel your acceptance, feel your excitement, feel how proud of him you are. When you speak to him, talk from that feeling place. If you tell him about the image you have of him in your mind, he will feel the acceptance in your voice. Tell him that you know this is the real man who is waiting to come out and ask him how you can support him in becoming that man.

- Practice curiosity. Begin by getting curious about everyday things—not just problems. You can ask your partner about work, his hobbies, or anything else that interests him. It doesn't matter what you get curious about at first, just ask questions and find out what gets him talking. Then paraphrase what he has said to see if you understand what is important to him. If he wonders why you are asking, just tell him you love him and want to be closer to him so you are doing a practice from the book you are reading. The more you get used to being curious when there's not a problem to dissect, the more natural it will seem to you when there is a bigger issue to examine.

Chapter 15

Love Your Sexuality

As a society, we tend to talk about sex a lot because quite frankly, compared to other aspects of our lives, it is more fun, more evocative, more scary, more personal, and more intimate—but mostly more fun. For you to truly *love* being you and living your life, you must learn to love your own sexuality and to feel the vibrancy of your own sexual energy. We are sexual beings. Sex is a part of our biological, emotional, and spiritual make-up. All of who we are is present when we make love—including all of our doubts, fears, resentments, old hurts, and personal quirks as well as all of our excitement, presence, confidence, and joys.

Our task is to bring *all* of who we are to *every* aspect of our lives, including sex. Because all of who we are is present in our sex lives, it's also true that all of what we do sexually can be seen as a metaphor for how we relate to each other and to ourselves. Do you express yourself fully with your partner, or do you hide part of yourself? Do you feel confident when you make love, or do you doubt your own worth as a lover and wonder if you are enough?

Most of the time, if both people in a couple are not fully satisfied sexually, they can trace the trouble to problems they are having outside the bedroom. In all the research, sexual satisfaction correlates highly with marital satisfaction; those of us who are happiest with our sex lives are also happiest with our partnerships. This does not mean that great sex leads to a satisfying marriage. It means that the couples who have the awareness and also the emotional and communication skills to have a great relationship probably also apply those same skills to their sexuality, their sexual energy, and their lovemaking.

The bottom line is this: In order to create sexual satisfaction that endures year after year, we must use all these skills, one moment at a time. *This* moment is the only one in which we can feel our sexual energy. So being fully satisfied sexually requires being fully present.

When our awareness is fully immersed in our sexual energy, we can't help but feel excited. And since sex, when done properly, puts us into direct contact with God, that awareness and that excitement promotes not only our physical well-being, but also our emotional and spiritual well-being. While some occasional disconnected sex can be really fun, sex goes best when both people are fully present and making emotional and spiritual contact as well as physical contact. That's why discovering what may be blocking us from fully embracing and fully expressing ourselves sexually is absolutely vital—it shows us what we need to heal in our lives.

Years ago, I witnessed a betrothal ritual that took place at the end of a powerful ceremony known as the Sun-Moon Dance. In the dance arbor, a line of cornmeal physically and energetically connects the arbor's east gate to the Tree of Life in the center. Although dancers are instructed not to cross this cornmeal line, the minister performing the betrothal ceremony stood right on top of the line. "God put some lines in our lives just so they would be more fun to cross," he said to the group. "Such is the line between women and men." This got a big laugh.

"I guess I'll never find out about that one," a lesbian woman standing behind me said loudly, which made the moment even funnier. Whether a sexual relationship involves a man and a woman, two women, or two men, it's the point of contact between the masculine and the feminine energies of each person that is exciting. Native American teachings explain that our sexual energy is the place where our masculine and feminine energies come together inside of us, just like it is the place where two people touch that feels so good sexually.

While men tend to carry more masculine traits and women tend to carry more feminine traits, these energies are not actually tied to gender. Each of us carries a combination of both masculine and feminine energy, no matter what our gender or sexual orientation. Masculine energy tends to be more action-oriented and physical, while feminine energy tends to be more receptive and emotional. We would all do well to carry a healthy balance of masculine and feminine energy, but not necessarily a 50/50 mix. Women (including straight women) can easily carry more masculine traits and men (including straight men) more feminine traits. Whatever your particular ratio, it's exactly right for you.

The relationships that work best are ones where both people find a healthy balance of masculine and feminine energies within themselves *and* between each other. Relationships get stale when only one person initiates sex or brings more energy to the lovemaking. We all need to be in that place of receiving from time to time, feeling our lover's excitement driving the activity. Each couple must find the balance that works specifically for them—and this usually involves some degree of taking turns being the initiator and the receiver. It keeps things fresh and new and exciting.

TRIPLE POINT

In thermodynamics, the term "triple point" refers to the temperature and pressure at which three phases of a substance (gas, liquid, and solid) coexist. So for example, if you have a container completely filled with water at the right temperature (273.16 degrees Kelvin) and the right atmospheric pressure (611.73 pascals), then ice, water, and water vapor will be present in the same place at the same time. A similar phenomenon happens with sexuality. When sex is at its best, you can feel three different energies—basal sexual energy, passionate emotional energy, and transformative spiritual energy—simultaneously.

Sometimes, couples can feel all three of these energies at once for extended periods, while at other times, these energies may flow rapidly from one phase to another, swinging from gentle, tender feelings of love with spontaneous bouts of silliness to energetic physical activity geared towards sexual pleasure to spiritual enlightenment, where one or both partners feel as if they are being held in the heart of God. All three of these energies are a part of our sexual make-up and it is important to embrace all of them if we are to stay fulfilled in our relationships.

So often, people feel very little sexual energy because emotional issues are throwing a wet blanket on libido. Although low sex drive is certainly common, it rarely occurs without some emotional factors being present that block sexual energy. In most cases, the sexual energy lights up as soon as the pressure from the emotional stressors is relieved.

Sexual Integrity

Chapter 12 talked about saying "yes" to all of who you are and saying "no" to who you are not. Sexual integrity is similar. It involves fully embracing your sexual energy and bringing all of it to your partner without holding back—as well as saying "no" to what does not serve your highest good.

When we become aware of our sexual energy on every level, we also become aware of the subtle ways that we can connect with each other and how those different subtle energies interplay with each other. A client named Vicki provides a good example. After working with me individually, she discovered that she had gone through what she called a "sexual growth spurt" where she became aware of her own presence in all areas of her life. She began feeling her own feelings and her own energy more and more. She loved feeling so alive and so connected with everyone with whom she came into contact. The problem came when she applied this same awareness to having sex with her husband, whom she described as a "typical, shut down man."

"I have discovered that it is possible to have sex, have an orgasm, and *not* be satisfied," Vicki told me. "Now, I want more. I want him to feel me. I don't think he can feel anything but his own dick. I want him to feel *all* of me. I want him to feel my heart and my soul. And dammit, I want to feel more of him, too!" Vicki had not merely gone through a sexual growth spurt, she had grown in a lot of areas in her life, and she was longing to connect more deeply and more thoroughly with her husband sexually. As Vicki discovered, as we grow in awareness, we quickly become dissatisfied with sexual contact that does not include being met spiritually and emotionally, as well as physically.

A lack of sexual integrity leads to an array of hurt feelings and pain ranging from the emptiness of emotionless sex to the trauma of perpetrator-victim encounters. If we were all aware of our sexuality on all levels and had no problem saying "no" to sexual contact in which we weren't met on every level, such pain would vanish because no one would be interested in any sexual contact that wasn't for the highest good. I know that's a tall order, and it's worth striving for.

Our society puts a premium on sexual attraction, paying little attention to emotional and spiritual compatibility, not to mention the degree to which someone can be present. The message we get in the media is that a sexual encounter with someone we're attracted to is the ultimate. This is a set up for dis-integrity because it ignores the emotional presence and spiritual awake-ness necessary for much more fulfilling and satisfying sex. While none of us deny that physical beauty is beautiful, few of us are taught the difference between sexual attraction and sexual chemistry. The questions we must ask ourselves about the people to whom we are attracted are, *How do all of our energies match? How emotionally open and available is this person?* and *How spiritually open is this person?*

As we begin to awaken to all of who we are and to all of what sex can be, our awareness raises the bar for our sexual expectations and sexual boundaries. Like Vicki, we are no longer satisfied by sexual contact in which we are not touched on every level. I like to think that humanity is on a path towards having sex with our entire beings, not just our genitals.

WHAT GETS IN THE WAY?

What gets in the way is trying to be something we are *not* and / or not being who we *are*—usually because of ignorance and hurt. Learning what it feels like to be open on every level is vital. So is healing your emotional hurts (including any kind of sexual trauma) so that you will feel safe enough to fully show up emotionally in sexual contact.

Chapter 12 discussed how we "should" on ourselves. We have all received messages about what we *should* do sexually, who we *should* be sexually, and what *should* be attractive to us. While some of these messages can be helpful, they may not fit for you. Your sexual energy is unique to you. If we try to apply another person's rules to our lives and they don't fit, we will constantly feel as if we are "shoulding" on ourselves.

One of the biggest "shoulds" that I hear about is desire. About 40 percent of my clients who "should" on themselves about their desire believe they should have more of it. Most of the time, people in this category are simply disconnected from their genuine desire because of some dynamic in the relationship or they have an emotional wounding around sex, belonging, or self-worth. Once the wound is healed, they begin to reconnect with their genuine desire again. The other 60 percent of my clients who bring up issues about their level of desire believe they shouldn't have the intense sexual desire that they have. Their work is to give themselves permission to be the highly sexual beings that they long to be.

The words "freak" and "freaky" are words people often use today to describe their sexuality. In fact, I have been surprised by how often the word "freak" comes up talking about sexuality and sexual desire. While "gettin' freaky" is slang for sexual intercourse and is certainly not meant as a negative, the word "freak" can carry both positive and negative connotations. Clients will often go back and forth between using "freak" to mean a person with a wild, wonderful, healthy, and incredibly high sex drive and using the same word in the same way to mean a person with a deviant, horrible, shamefully high sex drive.

If you have a high sex drive, it is imperative that you embrace it. There is nothing wrong with a high sex drive! A high sex drive is a problem *only* when you have a lack of integrity and engage in sexual activity that does not serve your highest good or support the highest good of another person. In this case, the problem is not having a high libido; it's the lack of integrity.

If you feel like a "freak" in the good way, then let yourself be a freak! If it is truly a part of who you are, then you need to embrace it and enjoy your sexuality. If you are staying in integrity on all the other levels of your being, you will keep yourself safe and bring nothing but the best to your partner. When you are embracing your sexuality authentically, you will be opening doors for yourself to higher levels of awareness emotionally, physically, and spiritually.

If you feel like a "freak" in the bad way, then you are either out of integrity or have some judgments around your sexuality that you need to work through. The lack of integrity, buried hurt, and what feel like the bad desires are pointing you towards healing those hurts. Either way, don't be scared of your desires. Your desire is either showing you who you genuinely are or showing you what needs to heal.

Whatever your genuine level of desire, it is exactly where it *should* be, so don't *should* on yourself about it. If you are not happy with your level of desire, you need to be really clear about why you want your desire to be different. In order to be in integrity, you have to embrace your level of desire exactly the way it is. If you ever try to be something you're not by forcing yourself to have more or less desire than you actually do have, then you are setting yourself up to be inauthentic with your partner. It is impossible to be fully present if you are, in essence, lying to yourself and to your partner about your level of desire.

He Wants You

Trust me ladies, your man wants you sexually, and you are enough just as you are. If your man is not showing his sexual desire, he is either disconnected from his own desire or he may be waiting for you to take the lead. The stereotype of men wanting and initiating sex more often than women is no longer accurate, if it was ever really true to begin with. Women express just as much desire as men, if not more. Gender stereotypes paint the picture of men with incredibly high sex drives and women who only agree to have sex after their men have worn them down. Women, you know this is not true. Not only do you have desire, you may have more desire than you feel it's okay to admit.

More than half the couples who come to me include women with higher sex drives who are more comfortable being the more sexually aggressive partner in their relationship. When couples experience discrepancies in desire, both are equally unhappy, whether it is the man or the woman who has the higher sex drive. Either way, the solution to resolving any tension that arises is the same: Accept yourself, accept your partner, and talk about it openly (even when you are scared, embarrassed, or triggered).

Many women who are naturally more sexually aggressive have learned to be more timid because a lot of men aren't okay with women having a stronger drive. The problem here isn't the woman's drive, it's her partner's displeasure with it. Men need to be okay with their own sexuality and know that they are every bit the lovers that they want to be. If they aren't, then they need to get professional help building confidence in their own sexuality. Of course, communication is the most important tool a couple can have when problems like this come up. Unfortunately, shame around their sex drive is one of the most common obstacles couples experience to embracing their desire and communicating it to each other.

THE SPIRITUAL ESSENCE OF SEX

The spiritual essence of sex for women involves embodying the Divine Goddess and bringing that energy into the world. When women allow the love of God to flow through them, this blesses their lovers; in the process, the women themselves open up and are also blessed with the love of God. Some theories say that over the last couple thousand years, the sacred feminine has been suppressed and those women who carry the sexual aspect of the divine feminine energy have been demonized. Whether you believe that or not is up to you. My hope for you is that you open yourself up enough emotionally, spiritually, and sexually to begin to formulate an opinion on the subject.

But not all women agree that this is the spiritual essence of sex for them. The others say the spiritual essence of sex is about safety. Some of these women have issues around safety (as discussed in Chapter 5), and for them, sex can be very comforting. Feeling their partner's masculine energy helps them feel protected, both emotionally and physically. For others in this camp, even the thought of sex evokes caution and makes them protectively pull in emotionally. Often, such women don't allow themselves to feel their own sexual energy, or at least not much of it. In the years I've been in practice, hundreds of women have come to me saying that they have no sex drive. When we dig a little deeper, we discover that they don't feel it's safe to feel their sexual energy—much less to let it out to share with someone else—because they feel they would never be supported or met in doing so, or that they would not be accepted. It is true that we all need to feel safe to open up, but safety is the first step. Safety is not the endgame; spiritual enlightenment is the endgame.

For men, the spiritual essence of sex is that during that moment of orgasm, they go into that sublime state of "no mind," where their awareness is completely wide open and they are completely in their senses, rather than in their heads. That is the moment of spiritual awakeness. In that split second—and for most men it is only a split second—they are open to God and to the healing powers that emotional and spiritual vulnerability can bring. This is true even for the most uber-macho, brain-dead, unenlightened men. The degree to which they pay attention, are open, and allow themselves to be vulnerable on the deepest levels is the degree to which they will be able to take that blessing into their lives and carry it with them. One of the biggest obstacles men face is in honoring the divine feminine in the women with whom they are involved.

LOVING WOMEN

Women, before you can love your sexuality, you have to love women because otherwise, you can't love yourself. This point is vital in finding happiness in relationships. The antithesis of loving women is being catty. We have all seen women get catty and gossip. Cattiness comes from one place—fear of not being enough. Cattiness is jealousy and it is an incredible hindrance to loving your sexuality.

In order to bring all of your sexuality to a relationship, you have to know your sexuality is good and you have to know your own beautiful radiance as a woman. If you cannot see beautiful feminine radiance in others, you cannot call it into your own life and love it in yourself. This principle is not only for women, but for men as well—they need to see not just a woman's physical beauty, but her feminine radiance, too. Men need to be able to love, adore, and appreciate women, as well as be secure enough within themselves to not be threatened by feminine radiance. Most often, the men who are threatened by the radiant beauty of powerful women are either insecure or are still carrying unhealed wounds. Such men either try to diminish women or they push them away, fearing the incredible power of the vulnerability that is possible in a relationship with an enlightened, empowered woman.

It's impossible to disrespect someone else unless you first learn to disrespect yourself. If you've been taught to respect yourself and to treat yourself respectfully, it will be the most natural and easy thing in the world to show respect to somebody else while still honoring yourself by setting appropriate boundaries.

How many times have you seen women getting catty with other women about men? Ladies, it's time to put that stuff to rest. What women need to be doing for the good of the planet is to come together and create a sisterhood where you are committed to raising the bar. A strong women's collective is necessary so that you're not competing for men but instead supporting each other for your mutual highest good and for the highest good of womankind. You'd also be developing your relationship skills so that you can inspire your men to be the greatest versions of themselves so that humanity as a whole can grow and evolve. Women, you are going to need to do this for all of us, because let's face it: Men aren't going to hold themselves to a higher standard of emotional intimacy by themselves.

Confidence is Sexy

Being okay with your own sexuality is vital. Whether you feel sexually confident or not, knowing that your sexuality is good is extremely important. You don't have to be the greatest lover in the world, all you have to do is accept yourself and be confident in your own presence. In fact, feeling and accepting your own sexual energy will breed confidence.

Ladies, confidence is the sexiest trait you can possess. If you struggle with shame, talk about it. If your man can support you, talk to him. If he can't, talk to a girlfriend who loves her own sexuality. Or talk to a therapist, but talk to someone. Don't hide your shame. Shining a light on it may be uncomfortable at first, but it's the only way to really examine it so that you can get rid of it for good. If you aren't willing to do that, your insecurity about your sexuality will hinder your ability to foster both sexual and emotional closeness with your partner.

GENDER DIFFERENCES

One gender difference comes up quite a bit with couples. While this is not applicable to all couples, it is common enough to mention. Some men need to have physical contact before they feel safe enough to open up emotionally, and some women need to have emotional contact before they feel safe enough to open up sexually. With couples who don't have good communication skills or who aren't good with getting in touch with their emotions, this just sounds like some kind of sick cosmic joke.

The way I see it, both men and women are called to understand and appreciate where the other person is coming from. We find each other because we need the gifts the other has to share with us. We are both called to have trust in our relationships so that we are not scared by this seemingly oppositional tendency. Ideally, in spiritual-emotional sex, the men receive the women's gift of emotionality and the women receive the men's gift of physicality. This unique exchange touches both people, and only when *other* needs are not being met does this dynamic feel unfair or lopsided.

PRACTICES:

- Practice fantasizing about your partner. (For some of you, this is nothing new.) Feel your desire and breathe into that feeling, allowing it to get bigger. Raise your tolerance for maintaining sexual excitement. See if you and your partner can turn each other on through talking, texting, and emails. See how much sexual excitement you can feel throughout the day.
- While fantasizing, if you constantly feel yourself getting distracted, you may need to develop some discipline to maintain focus. This may also indicate some internal objection, a need that is not being met, or some shameful voice inside. If you need something to allow your desire to come out, tell your partner. Open that discussion by saying that you want to bring more of your excitement to him or her, and you have noticed something getting in the way.

- Ask your partner for the chance to show each other what feels good. Take the time while having sex to check in with each other about what positions and techniques you most enjoy.

- Get comfortable using words. Don't rely on moans or heavier breathing to let your partner know what feels good. Say, "*yes!*" "I like that," or "Please don't stop." Don't be shy about what you love. Tell your partner clearly. If you are concerned he or she might not take what you have to say well, try, "I *love* that. Try it a little to the left. Yes, please don't stop."

- Practice pleasing each other with your hands. Give each other the gift of making some time that is all about the other. Men have been mastering the art of masturbation since puberty. We know every nuance of what feels good to us, and it is unreasonable to think that a woman will automatically know exactly what any particular man likes and needs. So women, keep checking in with your man about whether or not what you are doing feels good. Ask him, "Do you like *this* or do you like *this* better?"

- For men reading this book, I know you think you learned everything you need to know about sex by the time you were 15 years old, but trust me, there are a few things your woman needs you to know about *her*. She knows her body best, so let her teach you what feels good for her. Most men are insulted when women try to teach them about their bodies. But if you take a minute or two every now and then to let your woman guide you, you will end up feeling *great* about being able to please her more than you ever have before.

- Practice being sensual without having intercourse. Take a minute several times a day to flirt with your partner. Walk up behind your mate and kiss him or her on the neck and then walk off. Initiate a hug where your sole intention is to breathe your beloved in. Take a few seconds to look at and adore your partner and share how you feel. It feels good to do things like this to affirm your intimate connection, without having every contact turn into an initiation of full-blown sex.

Chapter 16

You Can Be Right or You Can Be Happy

About 99 percent of the arguments that couples bring into my office are people trying to prove that they are right (or that the other person is *not* right). But as we've discussed earlier, even if you *are* right, you *both* still lose when you argue like this because there's no hope for resolution. The true goal in any relationship is to be closer, to feel safe, to be seen, and to be fully present—being all of who you are in the union. When two people are trying to prove each other wrong, the issue is no longer about whatever they were talking about in the first place; the issue becomes in some way about self-worth, or being accepted. Usually, one or both people are not feeling heard or honored in some way.

This doesn't mean that they are not *actually* being heard or honored, it simply means that they are *feeling* that way, and that they are responding accordingly. The subconscious supposition going on is this: "If I can convince you that I am right, then I will know that you have heard me and honor me, and that means that I am not a bad person." Whenever self-worth feels at stake, it will supersede all other issues. A shift in perspective needs to happen in order for such a couple to begin softening their defenses and regain a cooperative, loving mindset.

I often think of an umbrella as a metaphor when couples argue. In a rain storm, you could argue about who gets to stand under the umbrella and you could both come up with some good points to make in the argument. The truth is that you need to put a big enough umbrella over your relationship to cover both of your needs. Trust in the communication process and trust in the power of authenticity is what provides an umbrella of sufficient size to cover both of your concerns and needs in your relationships. The umbrella of "being right" is only big enough to cover one person; the umbrella of authentic presence and compassionate listening will keep you both warm and dry through the harshest of storms.

As *A Course in Miracles* states: "The ego lives by comparison . . . The ego cannot survive without judgment . . . Love will immediately enter into any mind that truly wants it . . . Anger involves projection of separation, which must ultimately be accepted as one's own responsibility, rather than being blamed on others . . . The ego seeks to divide and separate. Spirit seeks to unify and heal."

In other words, arguments happen on the level of the ego, not on the level of the loving heart, and the ego is concerned only with its own worth. When people argue about who is right, it has the effect of saying, "I am a good person and you are bad."

If I feel as though you are calling me a bad person, then I am not going to *trust* you. I am going to defend myself. And I am not going to trust that my needs are going to be considered, so I must stop considering your needs to try to get my needs met.

This is when we get polarized, and the mindset becomes a "me vs. you" attitude. This whole defensive dance can be avoided through paying attention to when we get triggered, sharing only what we are feeling (and stating what we are feeling as feelings), and by listening compassionately even when we don't like what we are hearing.

WORLD-CLASS DEFLECTION AND BANTER GONE BAD: RODNEY AND SHERELL

Rodney and Sherell came into my office and sat on different sofas, which they generally didn't do. They didn't speak to each other as they settled in, and I sensed that they were *intentionally* not talking to each other. As I began to probe, an argument quickly erupted. I was able to record and transcribe the argument.

Both Rodney and Sherell are incredibly bright, well spoken, and very funny when they are not fighting. When the two of them begin to banter harshly, it can get heated pretty quickly. The conflicts escalate because neither of them is speaking or listening authentically. They're concerned only with their own feelings, not with what is important to the other.

The prime tactic that this couple used was casting doubt about the other's credibility, which landed with each of them as an affront to their self-worth. As you read the following transcript, see how many statements you can count that are attempts to discount the validity of what the other person is saying or to deflect responsibility onto or blame the other person.

The day before they came in, Rodney came home from work to find a new pair of pants and a blouse on hangers and covered in plastic placed across the back of the sofa. He and Sherell had an argument that she described as "bad" and they stopped talking to each other for the rest of the night and all of the following morning. The argument erupted in my office when Rodney said to his wife, "I can't believe you just bought a new outfit! We can't afford that right now!" Sherell let out a big, frustrated sigh.

"You played golf with your friends twice this week," she responded. "How much did that cost?"

"Yeah, but that's for work; I have to do that if I want to succeed at my job."

"You don't even deduct it from our taxes. How can it be for work?"

"You go out with your friends after work and discuss work stuff that you say needs to get done, and you don't deduct margaritas from your taxes. I don't even know what the standard deduction is for margaritas. We should call our accountant and ask her. That is if *you* didn't get us fired and we have to find a new accountant this year."

"I got us fired!? *I got us fired?!* Oh, Lord." Turning to me, Sherell asked, "Did you hear that?" Then she turned back to Rodney and continued: "She was laughing at you with all the crap you tried to deduct. 'Uh, I needed special shoe strings for my golf shoes,'" she said with a mocking tone. "'We had to special order them because I got the Italian leather shoes imported . . . from Italy.' Yeah, no shit, Sherlock. The Italian leather shoes were from Italy. She is a smart woman; I think she could have figured that one out. 'Oh, and my tailor hemmed my pants too short on all my suits, so I had to buy all new socks. I should deduct those too.'"

"Hey, when I am closing a big deal, I am not going to leave anything to chance," he countered. "You won't even listen to Jeffrey Fox [motivational speaker, high-power corporate consultant, and author of 11 best-selling business books, including *How to Become CEO* and *How to Become a Rainmaker*]. I take pride in doing things right, unlike you who just figured we would magically find the condo on Hilton Head last month without having even a clue where it was. 'Oh, it's Camelot or Cambridge or one of those places. I know where it is.' Meanwhile, we are sitting there for two hours waiting for your mom to drive to the house to find the paperwork in that mess you have made of the counter."

"The mess that *I* have made?!"

"Yeah, I don't even know what the counters look like in there, anymore."

"The mess that *I* have made. Right! Those are your bills, mister. Do you even know what things cost? Do you know what it takes to keep this family afloat? No. I didn't think so. Those are your bills on the counter. I am the one who pays them every month."

"You pay *some* of the bills," he said with a reprimanding tone. Then with a touch of haughty arrogance, he added, "There are plenty of things that I take care of that you don't ever have to worry about, including making the money."

In this interaction, both Rodney and Sherell are making massive, sweeping deflections in an attempt to discredit the point the other is trying to make. Such deflections constantly change the subject. I stopped them to ask, "Who's right?"

"About which part?" Sherell asked.

"About all of it," I said.

"I don't know. I guess I am, because I do pay some of the bills because I set up direct withdrawals," Rodney answered.

"Well, I guess since you set up direct withdrawals to pay some of the bills, you win the argument and are therefore vindicated in your claim that you guys can't afford for her to buy a new outfit," I said. Sherell busted out laughing.

"Yeah, I guess you are right," she said sarcastically. "We can't afford my new outfit for your awards ceremony, because two years ago, you gave someone our account number. OOOh, that's great!"

"I don't get it. What does one thing have to do with the other?" Rodney asked.

"That was my question," I interjected. "What does any of that have to do with her buying an outfit? What does her leaving the condo information on the counter have to do with buying an outfit?" I asked rhetorically.

"We had to sit at a restaurant for two hours ordering appetizers while her mom drove over to the house and found the papers on the counter to find out what condo we had rented," he tried to explain.

"I understand that," I said. "I am asking how it came up in a discussion about her new outfit."

"Honey, we do this all the time with each other," Sherell said. "Sometimes it starts off fun, but it gets bad. It gets real bad."

"Yeah, I know. I don't ever want it to get that way, but it just sort of happens."

I asked him to go back to the point when he walked in the door and saw her new outfit. "Press the pause button on that scene," I suggested.

"You are standing there, and you see a new outfit laying across the back of the couch. How do you feel in that very moment?"

He crumbled. He began to swat away tears and said, "I lost a big account."

"Oh God, honey! Which one?" Sherell asked. Rodney just kept shaking his head. "Was it the Statham account?" He nodded.

"Two things," he said next. "I was scared that she had spent too much money because I had just bought a new putter on the way home." When she heard this, Sherell laughed, adoring him—not judging him. "I shouldn't have bought it, I didn't need it, but I was feeling like hell." Then he looked at his wife with a half apologetic/ half embarrassed look and added, "The other thing was that I was hoping it was the outfit you had sent me the picture of last week when you were trying stuff on." He turned to me and said, "What can I say? My wife is hot! Especially in purple! But I couldn't remember if it was at Saks or at Macy's."

I summarized: "So instead of walking into the room and hugging her and saying, 'I am scared about money and feel like crap because I just lost a big account and bought a putter I don't need. Even though I am scared we can't afford it, I hope you bought that purple outfit you sent me the picture of last week, because you looked great in it,' you started yelling that you couldn't afford her outfit."

"I was going to get her to try it on for me later. Doesn't that make it okay?" he responded half-jokingly.

"There! You just did it with me," I said. "You just tried to discredit what I was saying. So are you saying that I am wrong? Or are you really saying, 'I am not a bad guy even though I was a jerk to my wife?'"

"Yeah, that. I don't want her to get fed up with me because I can be a jerk sometimes."

We talked about how their comments all revolved around deflecting blame, and how blame is an attack on self-worth. We talked about how whenever people perceive that their worth is threatened, they generally defend themselves without even being aware that it is their self-worth that they are defending.

Neither Sherell nor Rodney knew how the discussion had gotten to where it did. It wasn't until I played the audio recording back that I could even keep track of the string of topics in the minute or so of heated debate. I agreed to transcribe the short argument and gave them copies when they came back in the following week.

"Oh my gosh, we never even responded to what each other was saying, did we?" Sherell asked.

When they were finished looking over the transcription, Rodney said, "Wow, honey. You are really messed up. You need to work on this so you can quit messing up our relationship." It was obvious that he was joking, and she smiled and playfully hit him. She was about to respond, and I cut her off.

"Sherell, I want you to go ahead and respond to him however you were going to respond," I said. "But both of you pay attention to when it gets to where it is not fun anymore. So Rodney, make your smart-ass comment again." He did.

"I want you to take this to work," Sherell then said, holding up the transcription of their argument, "and show it to your assistant so she can see that she isn't the only one that has to put up with your sorry ass."

"Yeah, I'll do that if you take it to your tennis pro, and your masseuse, and your bikini waxer and do the same thing," Rodney said.

I saw her reaction to his comment and called time-out. "Are you still having fun with the witty marital banter?" I asked Sherrill. "Or are you ready to kick his ass right now?"

"That one stung a little," she admitted. "I wanna kick your ass," she said to him with an elevated pitch in her voice and accelerated speech. She was right at the point between joking and attacking.

"Sherell, which one of you is right?" I asked.

"It's not him," she said. "I don't have to kick his ass, because when his assistant sees how he talks to me, she is gonna kick his ass."

"Sherell, which one of you is right?" I asked again. She began tearing up.

"He is. I shouldn't spend all his money on tennis lessons and afternoons at the spa."

"Rodney, do you have a problem with her spending *all* your money at the spa? Is that what was behind your comment?" I asked.

"Oh goodness, no. Sweetie, you don't spend enough money on yourself. You are worth every penny. I am actually envious. It's *your* money, I'm just the one who makes it, and I want you to enjoy it."

"Now tell her how you were really feeling when you read the dialogue from last week," I suggested to him.

"I was really feeling: 'Dammit, sweetie. I am sorry I am such an asshole.' And I did it again just now. I am sorry."

With just a few exchanges in their dialogues, this couple can completely avoid a topic, ignore the chance for authentic contact, escalate the exchange to the point of anger, create a huge source of stress in their marriage, and destroy the good, loving feelings they have for each other. While they love each other very much and still have a quality to their relationship that is reminiscent of their high school love, they spend most every evening getting each other riled up. She ends up crying at least twice a week, and he drinks bourbon every night to help calm his nerves after coming home from his high-stress job and not getting any relief from that stress in their time together.

The task for this couple is twofold. The first piece is to recognize when they deflect to try to discredit the other person to make him or her wrong. The second piece is to recognize when someone's feelings get hurt during the course of their playful banter, which is meant to create intimacy. When feelings get hurt, it is time for the banter to stop and authentic communication to begin. When they were able to catch these two things when they first happened, their arguments stopped, the frustration began to evaporate, and they got to enjoy their deep connection quite a bit more again. They got to the place where they would stop arguing and one of them would make a feeling statement to get the topic of the conversation back on the course of closeness, authenticity, and enjoying the connection that gets lost when they argue.

FEELINGS VS. FACTS: CODY AND SHELLY

When Cody and Shelly came into my office, they sat on opposite ends of a couch and seemed as if they wanted to build a wall of throw pillows between them. They had been engaged for seven years and claimed that they fought all the time. Neither could really tell me what they fought about, which is common with some couples whose fights erupt out of reactivity rather than because of specific issues.

For Cody and Shelly, their reactivity *was* the issue they faced as a couple. They both suffered from low self-worth in different ways, and they were both frustrated with the relationship, although they loved each other very much. One of Shelly's chief complaints about Cody was that he shuts down and doesn't talk about his feelings.

One pattern of communication (or miscommunication) played out over and over with the two of them, and it not only contributed to but also escalated their fights and pretty much guaranteed that they wouldn't be able to solve their disagreements. The pattern was that each of them would argue with the other when the other made a feeling statement. One such fight erupted when Cody told me, "I feel like Shelly is mean to me and picks on me."

"That's just not true!" Shelly shot back instantly. She acted really hurt by Cody's statement. "I can't believe you would say that," she added, looking like a whipped puppy.

"Well, you *are* sometimes," Cody said. "Sometimes you say really mean things to me."

"No, I don't. I'm never mean to you. You're the one who is mean and yells at *me*," Shelly responded. And on it went, with the two of them arguing for quite a while, ignoring my attempts to redirect them. Eventually, we got to the bottom of what was going on. Shelly saw that she got triggered by Cody's feeling statement for two reasons. First, to her, it felt as if he was saying that she was a bad person (one of her "Am I Okay?" issues). Second, Shelly's mother was a horribly mean person and Shelly desperately wanted to avoid being like her mother. So when Cody said that he felt like she was mean to him, Shelly did what most of us do when we feel like our worth is attacked—she defended her worth by trying to discount what he was saying. The work for Shelly was to realize that if she wanted Cody to talk about his feelings, she needed to listen without arguing with him, *even when he shared something she didn't like.*

Cody was actually doing a good job of stating his feelings as feelings. He wasn't making a declaration or accusation such as, "You are mean to me." If he had said it that way, he really would have been insinuating that Shelly was a bad person because she hurt him, which would only make Shelly more defensive. But that isn't what he said here. Cody said he *felt* like she was mean to him—which was the truth. That's how he *felt*.

When Shelly took Cody's feeling statement as a statement of *fact*, she made a choice, without even being aware of it, to try to be right instead making the happy choice. The choice to be happy in this case would have been to get curious about why he was feeling the way he was and to empathize with him about how it must be for him to feel that way. Instead, Shelly chose to argue about whether or not he was right that she was mean – which in a way is changing the subject away from his feelings. By arguing about who is right, Shelly was ignoring Cody's pain—which just perpetuated the bad feelings and widened the emotional distance between them.

Here's the way out of this rabbit hole: If Shelly could accept that Cody felt like she was mean (regardless of whether or not she really *was* mean) and if she could empathize with what it must be like for him to feel that his fiancée was mean to him, then she would be able to take a step closer to him emotionally. In doing so, she could encourage him to continue sharing how he feels on a regular basis, helping him not to be so shut down.

Once I got Shelly and Cody both calmed down, I had Cody look Shelly in the eye and repeat his original statement, "I feel like you are mean to me."

In order to reinforce the "You can be right or you can be happy" principle, I had Shelly say, "While I don't think I am mean to you, I want to hear more about how you feel when you feel I am mean." Another way she could have responded would have been to say, "I know you feel that way, and I hate it that you feel that way. Tell me more about what it is like when you feel like I am mean."

When Shelly was able to listen to Cody share how he felt without arguing about whether he was right, he got a chance to expand on his feelings and then discover the hidden hurt behind those feelings. Cody shared that sometimes when Shelly talks to him, he feels severely criticized, and that's a trigger for him because he has historically felt like a loser and a horrible underachiever (both in his life and in his relationships). He added that once he started dating Shelly, he began feeling like a winner for the first time, because this amazing and talented woman loved him. His love for her made him feel like a loser again whenever she criticized him.

While Shelly had a hard time hearing these really good things about herself because of her own low self-worth, she was able to listen without arguing with Cody or discounting what he had to say. Shelly started to sniffle and sob while listening. She was touched by how important she was to him. She had finally listened long enough, without arguing, to hear him express his tender feelings for her and how grateful he was to have such an amazing woman in his life.

This is a perfect example of why focusing on being happy instead of being right is not a cop out. This principle isn't about sugarcoating situations. It's not about denying what's unpleasant or playing Pollyanna by trying to look on the bright side. It's about being willing to walk through the darkness of our own fears in order to get to the light of love. It's about being able to see the forest for the trees, or perhaps in this case, being able to see the amazingly colorful and exotic tropical rainforest for all the weeds.

PRACTICES:

- Make "I feel" statements instead of making accusations. Your feeling statement is about you, it isn't about your partner, so there's no argument to be had. The idea is to share authentically how you are feeling in the moment ("I feel hurt") without insinuating an attack on the other person ("You hurt me" or "You are mean"). When you need to pinpoint when the feelings occurred say, "When you did _____, I felt _____." This works because your partner is more likely to have compassion for how you feel if you do not insinuate that your hurt is his or her fault.

- When your partner says that you have hurt him or her, simply respond, "I know you are hurt. I don't want you to hurt." You will be amazed at how disarming this can be.
- Be attentive to worth and to how you communicate your worth (and the worth of the person with whom you are talking). Notice when you feel your worth is threatened or when you start to defend yourself or your actions. When you notice that, *celebrate* your growing awareness by saying to your partner, "Hey, I just caught myself getting defensive. I was going to say something because I didn't want you to think I was a jerk. I am sorry. I want to hear what you are saying. Tell me again." Every time you catch yourself, you'll get closer to stopping the cycle of dysfunction for good.

* * *

You were born to have an amazing life and you were given a heart that longs to love greatly. Love is easy, and it flows quickly and abundantly unless you do something to block its flow. Chances are you weren't taught the mindset or the emotional and communication skills necessary to keep the channel of love wide open and flowing in your relationships. But now that you've read this book, you are well on your way to mastering these skills.

When you are able to acknowledge your hurts and respond genuinely when you get triggered; when you can make space for your loved ones when they get triggered without getting triggered yourself; when you can listen not only to the words your beloved shares, but to what is underneath his or her words; when you can embrace the greatest version of yourself as well as of others; and when you can remember that intimacy is your first priority in your relationships; then you are setting yourself firmly on the path of not only having awesome relationships, but also living a life rich with enlightened authenticity. Bless you.

About the Author

Marcus Ambrester, M.A., was born in Texas and raised in Knoxville, Tennessee. He earned a bachelor's degree in psychology and speech communication from the University of Tennessee, and in 2004, he received his master's degree in transpersonal counseling psychology from Naropa University in Boulder, Colorado. He is an ordained minister and has worked extensively with Native American and Yogic healing modalities for the past 15 years.

While living in Boulder, Marcus worked with Vietnam Veterans and their wives. He taught classes on alcoholism recovery to people convicted of DUIs and worked in private practice with the Niwot Center for Integrative Therapies (now Colorado Therapies). In addition, he's worked with his wife Jennilea leading four-day spiritual retreats for couples.

In 2006, Marcus returned to Tennessee to open a private practice in Nashville. His counseling practice focuses on couples who started off with a great connection and over time feel like their connection has either been lost or buried under a mountain of hurt, frustration, anger, and resentment. He also counsels women who are frustrated with where their lives are headed, scared there is something wrong with them, and overwhelmed that nothing seems to help. In short, Marcus coaches people to find and resolve the blocks that prevent them from walking their life's path with happiness, abundance, and joy.

ACKNOWLEDGMENTS

I want to acknowledge several people for their contributions not only to this book, but also for their contributions to my life. First off is my wife, Jennilea. You have been the personification of loving support throughout our marriage and especially throughout the writing and publishing of this book. All the times I shut the door in order to make a deadline were met with nothing but support and encouragement. I think your memoirs would be a better example for people on how to make awesome relationships than this book could ever be. You are a jewel and I am thankful to get to call you my own.

Bug and Jo, bless you two sweet souls. I am sorry daddy has had to work so much to finish this little project of mine. As I have worked on this book, you have each written so many books, too. It has been an honor to help and a joy to watch. I hope the two of you know how much I love you and how adorable the two of you really are.

Celia and Roy Ambrester, You provided the space for me to discover this path and these teachings. Mom, I love you and am so thankful for your presence in my life. Pops, I had hoped you would live to see this book in print, and thank you for overseeing it from there.

Grandpa Joseph, you followed your vision to bring your work to the people who were hungry for it. You broke a lot of rules and took a lot of heat in order to open the door that you opened for all of us. Thank you!

Grandpa Benito, I love you and I Bless you. Thank you for that lesson . . . and all the others. Remember that tractor song!

Cheryl Rose, Thank you for walking me through the darkness in which I had found myself and teaching me how to find that quiet place inside that shines the light of Spirit.

Steve Citty, thank you for seeing me. Thank you for seeing the man I am capable of being instead of the man that I was. Thank you for being so patient with me. You are UncleGrandpa, I can't wait to see what the next 16 years hold.

Duey Freeman, you are a true master. You bring a depth of presence that is unrivaled.

John Pehrson, you have been such an inspiration to me and instilled in me a drive to be of service to the people by showing me what it is like to let go of any sense of security in order to do what is right. You . . . You got a gift, You!

Jeanne White Eagle, you show up in the world without any hesitation or reservation. While you were blessed with one of the greatest singing voices on the planet, your real legacy is in showing us all how important *our* voices are.

John Stroupe & Mike Wollard, I group you two together because you took me under your wings together. You protected me during a critical time of growth while at the same time honoring me as the man you knew I could be. You are incredible men. Thank you for your service to the people.

Beth Young, your support during the writing of this book was amazing; you never failed to help me get back to that place where the magic would flow.

Tripp Lanier, you reached out and began pointing me in the right direction when I was crumbling. Thank you, brother. You will never know the difference you made.

Robbie & Teresa, I don't know how it happened, but the two of you provided a foundation in my life I had always dreamed of.

John, Alyson, Rob, & Nataraja, I wouldn't have made it without you. Bless you all.

Allison Keeley, your continued support and guidance is such a gift. You have one of the most inspiring ways of kicking a person in the ass! You are a gift to the planet.

Adam Markel, you are living it, thanks for showing me what it looks like.

Eric Frady, you put the fear of God in me, without even realizing it. I made my deadline.

Made in the USA
San Bernardino, CA
24 September 2014